A revolutionary and life-shaping book on kingdom leadership, one rooted not in outcome-based theories about leadership but in theology — a kingdom-saturated and gospel-based theology where the leader is first a follower whose character is transformed by God's grace. The revolution of this book is that God's transformation of us makes us God's kingdom leaders, and this is just the kind of leadership we need today. Five stars!

SCOT MCKNIGHT, Professor of New Testament, Northern Seminary

Joe knows leadership. And he knows what the Bible says about leading. He's a guide worth following.

JOHN ORTBERG, Senior Pastor of Menlo Park Presbyterian Church and author of *Who Is This Man?*

This book is powerful. It exposes the eternal consequences of having earthly applause for our Christian leadership and service, while receiving Heaven's silence. And it is incredibly encouraging because it also reveals that leaders and ministries that seem to have earth's silence may one day be the very ones who receive Heaven's applause. After reading it, I re-examined my leadership, repented of my desire for "outcome," and recommitted my "followership" to more clearly reflect our Servant King. Thank you, Joe Stowell.

ANNE GRAHAM LOTZ, Speaker and author of *Wounded by God's People*

My soul needed this book. *Redefining Leadership* offers the profound reminder that our legacy is formed by who we are, and not merely by what we accomplish.

JEFF MANION, Senior Teaching Pastor, Ada Bible Church in Ada, Michigan, and author of *The Land Between*

I am so grateful to God that my dear friend, Joe Stowell, has written *Redefining Leadership*. Not only is Joe a portrait of what he has written, but he has also spent much of his life and ministry shaping the next generation of Kingdom leaders. He writes not just from experience and what he has observed, but from a life and ministry marked by godly integrity. This book is a treasure and should be required reading for every Christian leader and all who have been given the gift and privilege of influencing others. Thanks, Joe, for the clear, compelling reminder that we are to lead according to the ways of the Kingdom and the will of our King, Jesus Christ.

Dr. Crawford W. Loritts Jr., Author, speaker, radio host, and senior pastor of Fellowship Bible Church, Roswell, Georgia

REDEFINING
LEADERSHIP

Other Books by Joseph Stowell

Following Christ

Loving Christ

Radical Reliance

Revelation
(Great Books of the Bible Series)

Simply Jesus and You

The Trouble with Jesus

REDEFINING LEADERSHIP

CHARACTER-DRIVEN HABITS OF EFFECTIVE LEADERS

JOSEPH M. STOWELL

ZONDERVAN

Redefining Leadership
Copyright © 2014 by Joseph M. Stowell

This title is also available as a Zondervan ebook.
Visit www.zondervan.com/ebooks.

This title is also available in a Zondervan audio edition.
Visit www.zondervan.fm.

Requests for information should be addressed to:

Zondervan, 3900 *Sparks Dr. SE Grand Rapids, Michigan 49546*

Library of Congress Cataloging-in-Publication Data

Stowell, Joseph M.
    Redefining leadership : character-driven habits of effective leaders / Joseph M. Stowell.
        p. cm.
    ISBN 978 - 0 - 310 - 21565 - 3 (hardcover jacketed)
    1. Leadership — Religious aspects — Christianity. I. Title.
BV4597.53.L43S77 2014
658.4'092 — dc23   2013030217

All Scripture quotations, unless otherwise indicated, are taken from *The Holy Bible, English Standard Version,* copyright © 2001 by Good News Publishers. Used by permission. All rights reserved.

Scripture quotations marked NIV are taken from The Holy Bible, *New International Version®,* NIV®. Copyright © 1973, 1978, 1984, 2011 by Biblica, Inc.® Used by permission of Zondervan. All rights reserved worldwide.

Scripture quotations marked KJV are from the King James Version of the Bible.

Any Internet addresses (websites, blogs, etc.) and telephone numbers in this book are offered as a resource. They are not intended in any way to be or imply an endorsement by Zondervan, nor does Zondervan vouch for the content of these sites and numbers for the life of this book.

Cover design: Studio Gearbox
Cover photography: Veer
Interior design: Ben Fetterley and Greg Johnson/Textbook Perfect
Interior composition: Greg Johnson/Textbook Perfect

Printed in the United States of America

14 15 16 17 18 /DCI/ 22 21 20 19 18 17 16 15 14 13 12 11 10 9 8 7 6 5 4 3 2 1

To Joe, Matt, and Rod ...
My sons and son-in-law, whose lives exemplify
the best of character-driven leadership

"A wise son brings joy to his father."
(PROVERBS 10:1)

CONTENTS

IN GRATITUDE

I am well aware that without supportive influencers in my life, a book like this — or anything else for that matter — would be impossible. At the top of my list of influential people in my life is Martie, who has graciously shared her life journey with me. Martie has been a constant source of encouragement and support. Her wise and discerning insights have guided and groomed me in so many productive ways. In fact, those of you who know her will hear her voice in many of the thoughts in the book. I am forever thankful that she is such a faithful friend.

Beth Longjohn, my executive assistant, organizes my work life with class and efficiency. Her gifted partnership helps me clear space in my life to pursue the ministry of writing. Thanks, Beth!

I am grateful as well for the good folk at Zondervan who kept after me to get these thoughts in print and their Job-like patience with how long it took to finish the manuscript. The Z team is a great example of how publishers should partner with authors. Thanks to Ryan Pazdur, who early on encouraged and guided me in the development of my thoughts, and to Jim Ruark for his excellent work in helping to wrap up the project.

Mostly, I am thankful to our Lord, whose Word gave me a foundation from which to write and who by his grace gave me gifts that empowered the process. To him be the glory!

A REDEFINED GOAL

A Life Well Lived

In conversations about leadership, I am most frequently asked, "What's your biggest challenge?"

My answer is always, "Me!"

That's not to say that I haven't faced other daunting challenges. It's just to admit that even in the midst of those challenges, the most important issue is, "How am I managing myself through the situation?" Will anger, manipulation, compromise of integrity, plotting for self-preservation, pessimism, despair, shifting the blame, self-pity, or covering up be valid options? Or, in good times will posturing myself to take the credit, seeking the affirmation and applause of others, thinking too well of myself, or ignoring the contribution that others have made characterize my response?

This book is about the challenge of "me" in leadership. So, if you are looking for a book on management strategies, team building, assessment, goals and objectives, or branding and growth strategies, then this is probably not the book for you. Although, if that is what you are still looking for as a leader, this may be exactly the book you should be reading. If, however, you have come to realize that the *kind of person you are* and *how you navigate your leadership* is at the core of long-term effectiveness, then join me as one who is passionate about leading the right way for maximum outcomes by getting "me" in sync with the counterintuitive, countercultural ways of the world's most unlikely leader, Jesus Christ.

Redefining Leadership aims to draw you as a leader to a character-driven leadership experience that will produce maximum outcomes. Leaders who shortcut the process and lead simply for great outcomes, with little regard for who they are and how they lead, will ultimately produce minimum outcomes and discount their legacy as a leader. My intention is not to denigrate those who lead merely for outcomes (though I would like to encourage them to rethink the tipping point of character in their leadership), but to make character-driven leadership an intriguing, compelling, and biblically necessary option.

THE TARGET

All of us are uniquely wired. Our wiring consists of a special combination of gifts, temperament, and personality that have been given to us by God and influenced by both the culture in which we have grown up and the impact of influential people in our lives. Thankfully, there is no "cookie cutter" pattern for the ideal leader profile. If we were all the same, someone would be unnecessary.

But in our God-woven uniqueness there is a singular target toward which we should all be taking aim. That target is the character-driven patterns and principles of effective leadership that are charted for us in the ways of the Kingdom and the will of our King, Jesus Christ. These non-negotiable principles take on an array of applications that are uniquely expressed through our styles and differences. But in our uniqueness we must never compromise the essentials of kingdom leadership. Leaders who celebrate their uniqueness yet ignore character flaws by saying, "That's just who I am," forfeit the privilege of forward movement toward maximum leadership. They miss the target.

My friend Erwin Lutzer, longtime pastor of The Moody Church in Chicago, tells the story of a town wag who shot an arrow at the side of his barn and then painted a target around it, with his arrow smackdab in the middle.... Bulls-eye! Leaders who perceive that successful leadership rises or falls singularly on the outcomes they generate have painted the bulls-eye around their own arrow. Character-driven leadership, by contrast, is a target that Christ has painted on the barn of our calling, and the issue is whether or not we are willing to aim our leadership toward his bulls-eye.

THE LEADERSHIP CHOICE

In the following pages we will discuss two kinds of leaders: *Outcome-Driven Leaders* and *Character-Driven Leaders*. Outcome-driven leaders focus primarily on maximizing outcomes. Character-driven leaders, while committed to good outcomes, believe that Leadership 101 is about the kind of person they are as they lead and how they lead. They focus on the development of character and the embracing of kingdom principles as a necessary first step in effective leadership.

The distance between the two leadership styles is significant. And the choice as to which kind of leader we will be is critical. Very few leaders completely exemplify either category at the extremes; in fact, I have never met a leader who is the perfect example of either end of the spectrum. But all leaders will land somewhere on the continuum between the two. So the issue is not whether or not I am the poster child for one or the other, but rather in which direction my life and leadership are headed.

So, to know where we fall on the continuum and in what direction we are headed, let's look at the characteristics of each approach. (See chart on page 16.)

INSTINCTIVE LEADERSHIP

If your trajectory seems to be headed toward outcome-driven leadership don't be surprised. The attraction to the convenience of discounting character for immediate outcomes is rooted in the early history of our race. In the beginning, God created Adam and Eve to enjoy an unhindered relationship with him, to find pleasure in each other, and to steward the beautiful and beneficial environment in which they were placed. They were the best kind of people who flourished in a surrendered fellowship with their Creator-God. Their stewarding leadership of the environment made it a place of harmony and unstained beauty. And their satisfaction

OUTCOME-DRIVEN LEADERSHIP Instinctive Leaders	CHARACTER-DRIVEN LEADERSHIP Kingdom Leaders
Identify themselves as leaders	Identify themselves as followers
Measure their success by outcomes	Measure their success by the positive influence of their character and leadership style on the people who generate the outcomes.
Use people to build the enterprise	Use the enterprise to build people
Promote themselves as the indispensable center of the organization	Elevate Jesus as the indispensable center
Believe that the organization should serve them and their interests	Believe that they are there to serve the best interests of the organization, its people, and its outcomes
Lead with the power of positional authority	Lead with the power of moral authority
Demand and posture for affirmation and personal recognition from the constituencies of the organization	Willingly affirm others to lead for the ultimate affirmation of hearing "Well done, good and faithful servant"
Trust their own instincts	Know their fallenness, are unsure of their instincts, and willingly rely on the wisdom of Jesus and godly counsel
Are competitive	Energetically cooperate with others for the advancement of the work of Christ
See themselves as a CEO	See themselves as a shepherd

came from managing the enterprise where God had placed them for his glory and pleasure.

Until!

Until they were tempted to focus on themselves rather than on their God. Until they fell to the seductive allure of self-fulfilling outcomes. So they took the forbidden fruit and infused into the human DNA a propensity to live for seemingly bigger, better, and more self-fulfilling outcomes while ignoring what kind of people they are becoming in the process. No wonder we drift toward self-serving outcomes in leadership. It's under our skin. It's instinctive.

As children of the fall, we are faulted to the core. This means that leading by our own instincts, no matter how well they seem to serve us and our outcomes, may cause us to lead in all the wrong ways. I came to realize long ago that given my fallenness, my first instincts are most likely wrong. I don't naturally like to pass the credit on to deserving others. I don't forgive freely. I don't like criticism and often respond poorly. When negative things happen, I tend to resist them instead of accepting them as reproof and an opportunity to learn. I like to think that I can be self-confident and self-reliant. I tend to think too well of myself. The list goes on.

So, by experience I have come to learn how desperately dependent I must be on the leadership of the King and the principles of the kingdom to get leadership right. But beware! Because of our own inherent twistedness, the kingdom way will often seem counterintuitive, pragmatically unproductive, and upside down. Yet, if the leadership recommendations of Jesus seem upside down, think again. They seem that way because in actuality *we* are upside down. Jesus is, always is, right-side up!

It's like toast in the morning. You slather it with butter and pile on the jam, and as you walk to the table, it slides off the plate and lands on the floor ... always upside down. It's a mess. Like upside-down toast, we tend to make a mess of things when left to ourselves. Then Jesus comes as the divine spatula and scrapes us off the floor of our fallenness and turns us right-side up. Effective leaders welcome Jesus into the mess and get right-side up with him!

REMEMBERING WHO WE ARE

At the core of our faulted outcome-driven view of leadership is a fundamental oversight. The oversight is that we have forgotten who we have become in Christ — that as leaders we are first and foremost followers of Jesus and as such that we are citizens of his kingdom. We are called to be loyal followers who not only live by, but also lead by the standards of the kingdom for the fame and glory of the King. The apostle Paul reminds us that we have been rescued from the domain of darkness and have been transplanted into the kingdom of Christ (Col. 1:13). The domain of darkness is managed and manipulated by a fallen set of assumptions and a wrong-headed set of values — values that prioritize outcomes over character. Leading by the earthside instincts of leadership is a denial of our fundamental identity. If we by redemption are kingdom people and followers of the King, then we must lead as such.

It's our upside-down-ness that leads us to think that successful leaders are measured by the size and scope of the enterprise, its branding, its national and even international acclaim, its profitability, the fame and platform of the leader. It may be assumed that since she is a successful leader, her life and leadership are in good order. Otherwise, why would God let her succeed? Wrong assumption! Or, if it's known that the leader is less than exemplary and has cut corners of integrity to accelerate success, it is often excused, since "God is certainly blessing the work." Wrong again! He may be blessing the work, but that's not the issue. The issue is Jesus' interest in who the leader is at the core and how he or she is leading as a steward of the work of the kingdom.

A LIFE WELL LIVED

Kingdom leadership, the character-driven kind, is measured by the life of a leader who cuts a wide and impactful swath of positive influence because of who they are as a leader and how they lead. It's the power of a life well lived. When he ushered in his kingdom, Jesus inaugurated a new way. He called for leaders to follow him and, as such, influence and motivate their followers toward personal, spiritual, communal, and organizational growth. Leaders who lead as followers of Jesus lead with the power of moral authority. And this highly leveraged leadership approach is available to all, even to those who may at first glance seem to be unlikely leaders.

Mother Teresa was an unlikely leader. She was a smallframed, bent-over nun who gave herself to serve the slum people of New Delhi in India. Asked to speak at the National Prayer Breakfast in Washington, D.C., she delivered a powerful defense of valuing the life of the unborn. Hardly able to see over the podium, she courageously articulated the importance of protecting life. As she spoke, two of the most powerful leaders in the world — President Bill Clinton and Vice President Al Gore — were seated on either side of her. Both of them were outspoken advocates of abortion.

She said,

> I feel that the greatest destroyer of peace today is abortion, because it is a war against the child, a direct killing of the innocent child, murder by the mother herself.
>
> And if we accept that a mother can kill even her own child, how can we tell other people not to kill one another? How do we persuade a woman not to have an abortion? As always, we must persuade her with love, and we remind ourselves that love means to be willing to give until it hurts. Jesus gave even his life to love us. So the mother who is thinking of abortion should be helped to love — that is, to give until it hurts her plans or her free time — to respect the life of her child. The father of that child, whoever he is, must also give until it hurts.
>
> By abortion, the mother does not learn to love, but kills even her own child to solve her problems. And, by abortion, the father is told that he does not have to take any responsibility at all for the child he has brought into the world. That father is likely to put other women into the same trouble. So abortion just leads to more abortion.
>
> Any country that accepts abortion is not teaching its people to love, but to use any violence to get what they want. This is why the greatest destroyer of love and peace is abortion (National Prayer Breakfast, February 3, 1994).

The statement drew a standing ovation.

Needless to say, her comments created a rather awkward moment for the President whose speech followed directly on the heels of Mother Teresa's. When he began his speech, he said, "It's hard to argue with a life so well lived!"

A life well lived gives power and credibility to even unlikely leaders and maximizes the outcomes of their service. A leadership life that is well lived is the goal of every character-driven leader. And character-driven leaders believe that Paul's words to the Colossians are defining targets for their leadership:

> Put on then, as God's chosen ones, holy and beloved, compassionate hearts, kindness, humility, meekness, and patience, bearing with one

another and, if one has a complaint against another, forgiving each other; as the Lord has forgiven you, so you also must forgive. And above all these put on love, which binds everything together in perfect harmony. And let the peace of Christ rule in your hearts, to which indeed you were called in one body. And be thankful. Let the word of Christ dwell in you richly, teaching and admonishing one another in all wisdom, singing psalms and hymns and spiritual songs, with thankfulness in your hearts to God. And whatever you do, in word or deed, do everything in the name of the Lord Jesus, giving thanks to God the Father through him (Col. 3:12 – 17).

PART 1

A REDEFINED PRIORITY

Character Counts

CHAPTER 1

CHARACTER-DRIVEN LEADERSHIP

The Tipping Point

What if?

What if leaders who from outward appearances seem to be successful turn out not to be successful in the end? What if leaders who seem outwardly less than successful turn out, in the long run, to be the most effective? What if effective leadership is not just about casting vision, setting goals, and motivating minions to accomplish those goals? What if there is more to good leadership than the building of great enterprises and the glory of the leader? What if the applause of this world for leaders stands in sharp contrast to a deafening silence in heaven?

Leadership is a lot like life ... it's all about the definitions. Get the definitions right and you get *life* right. Or in this case, define leadership correctly and you get leadership right. Get the definitions wrong and you get leadership wrong. In one of my favorite cartoon strips, *The Wizard of Id*, the king is sitting on the throne and his right-hand guy whispers in his ear, "Rodney is outside with a wagon full of underwear." To which the king replies, "Give me strength. All I asked Rodney to do was to debrief his troops!" How we define leadership and measure success will determine whether or not in the end we are standing there with a proverbial wagon load of underwear.

So let's start.

WHAT KIND OF LEADER?

As we have noted, there are fundamentally two kinds of leaders.

There are **Outcome-Driven Leaders,** whose primary focus is on *motivating others to achieve great organizational outcomes.* Although they are often able to produce stellar results for a time, the narrowness of their focus ultimately diminishes the breadth and long-term effectiveness of their leadership. The power of their leadership is leveraged by the authority of their position instead of the credibility of their lives.

Or, there are **Character-Driven Leaders,** whose *exemplary lives influence and empower those within the sphere of their authority to achieve great outcomes personally, spiritually, communally, and organizationally.* The breadth and depth of their positive influence distinguishes them as *maximum leaders.* The power behind their leadership is leveraged by their moral authority that comes from the credibility of their lives. And, among other things, character-driven leaders use their organization to build stellar people, who in turn build a thriving culture that produces maximum corporate outcomes to the fame and glory of God.

Leaders must make the choice as to what kind of leader they will be.

THE CHOICES YOU MAKE

I have a friend who gave me a great piece of advice. He said, "Joe, your life is not made by the dreams you dream but by the choices that you make." The same is true of our leadership. It is not the dreams we dream about being a leader, but about the choices we make that will determine what kind of leader we will be.

Leadership is a gift. Stewarding that gift is a privileged responsibility for which we will be held accountable. And the choices we make in regard to how we steward the gift are strategic. There are three pivotal choices.

Choice #1 *is whether or not you are willing to choose character as the* *defining priority of your leadership.* Whether or not you believe that character counts. That if given a choice, character trumps outcomes.

Choice #2 *is whether or not you will choose "follower" as your leadership identity.* Whether or not your leadership will be shaped by following the will, ways, and wisdom of Jesus or by your own instincts.

Choice #3 *is whether or not you will lead with the counterintuitive competencies of the kingdom of Christ or with the normative ways of earthside leadership advice.*

Your choices will be determined by your personal perspectives as a leader. If you lead solely from a strong sense of self-confidence and a belief in the validity of your own instincts, if you are a follower of the normative earthside advice about leadership, you are most likely to define your leadership by its outcomes. By contrast, if you understand your own fallenness and the need to find your confidence in Christ and his counterintuitive, countercultural ways, and if it's your desire to bring the values of the kingdom to bear on your leadership and those you lead, you have a good chance of choosing the maximum successes of character-driven leadership.

DEFINING SUCCESS

In reading most leadership literature, it would be easy to conclude that success is measured by the outcomes that the leader is able to produce. Successful leaders are most often measured by the size and scope of the enterprise — its branding, its national recognition, its profitability, and at times the notoriety of the leader. No questions asked!

But what if there is more at the core of successful leadership, particularly for spiritual leaders, than the mere accomplishment of organizational goals, the growth of an enterprise, and the name recognition of the leader?

What if making the right choices about *how you lead and who you are as you lead; who you will follow as you lead, and what kind of competencies you lead with* are "first step" defining measurements of successful leadership?

The biography of Steve Jobs, founder of Apple, Inc., demonstrates that it is possible for a leader to generate amazing outcomes regardless of exemplary character traits. I am a direct beneficiary of Jobs's technological genius. I am typing this manuscript on my MacAir while listening to my favorite music on my iPad and waiting for the ding-ding of my iPhone to alert me to incoming emails and texts. Clearly, Jobs exemplified the kind of leadership that generates world-changing outcomes. His leadership at Apple redefined our culture and transformed the way millions of people live.

Yet there were incidents in Jobs's life that reflect a tendency to lead more by expediency than by virtue. His biographer, Walter Isaacson, when itemizing Jobs's propensity to permit outcomes to trump character, writes,

> Jobs sometimes avoided the truth. Helmut Sonnenfeldt once said of Henry Kissinger, "He lies not because it's in his best interest, he lies because it's in his nature." It was in Jobs' nature to mislead or be secretive when he felt it was warranted.... ordinary rules didn't apply to him.[1]

Even if a case were to be made that in the larger picture of corporate competition character is not all that important and that outcomes are indeed the ultimate endgame of success, particularly to the stockholders, it would be impossible to defend that position when we are talking about the kingdom enterprise. Running the kingdom by earthside standards is a contradiction of the very nature of the kingdom itself. Kingdom success is measured by conformity to the will and ways of the King and the maturing of his bride, the people we lead. Character-driven leaders agree with my pastor friend, Jeff Manion, who pastors a flourishing church in West Michigan. Jeff told me that when he dies, he wants his leadership to be worthy of writing "He was faithful to the Bride" on his gravestone.

If someone were to write your biography, would you be satisfied to have them celebrate your accomplishments while reflecting poorly on your character? Or would you rather have them positively underscore the kind of exemplary person you were as you led the Bride of Christ?

What I find interesting is that most often outcome-driven leaders get a hall pass on character if the results of their leadership are significant. I hear comments such as, "Well, I wouldn't want to be like her, but she knows how to get the job done." Or, more troubling yet, "I'm not sure I would want my son to be like him, but God is really using him." Observations like these reveal a dangerously faulted perspective on leadership. In essence, they reflect the belief that outcomes trump character and that

---

1. Walter Isaacson, *Steve Jobs* (New York: Simon & Schuster, 2013), 579.

what a person produces is the most important value in measuring successful leadership.

What we need to realize is that if a leader has achieved great outcomes but has failed to be exemplary and as such has failed to have a positive influence on the people, culture, organization, and town — or worse yet, has had a debilitating effect on the lives of those they have led, the organization they have served, or the community in which they have been placed — then from God's perspective there is something seriously out of sync in their leadership, regardless of the outcomes.

Warning! If you believe leadership is ultimately measured by how well you can deliver the goods, then in the end you will fail in your calling as a leader.

It should not go unnoticed that the greatest leader to have ever lived did not achieve immediate success in terms of outcomes. He was not highly networked, was disenfranchised from the powerful and the elite, was rejected by men, was poor and itinerant, and in the eyes of even his closest followers seemed a failure. Yet, who he was and how he led was a magnet to the masses, and to this day his leadership is heralded and admired for the way in which he led and the example of the life that he lived as he led. And the outcomes? He has left a legacy that has lasted far beyond his lifetime and has influenced generations for the last two thousand years … generations who so admire him that they adopt his ways to the extent of being willing to die for him if necessary.

CHARACTER COUNTS

Consistently, Scripture calls us to choose *character-driven leadership*. In the story of the ten talents, those who successfully stewarded the master's estate were rewarded with this character-affirming declaration: *"Well done, good and faithful servant!"* While outcomes are not unimportant in the story, the affirmation is about the character of the steward that produced the outcomes — affirmation about who the steward is (*"good and faithful"*) and an affirmation about how the steward leads (*"servant,"* Matt. 25:14 – 30).

Paul himself was aware of the priority of character as a leader. Comparing his leadership to a race, he concludes that winning the race rises and falls on the issue of character. Citing the character qualities of self-control and personal discipline, he concludes, "... lest after preaching to others I myself should be disqualified" (1 Cor. 9:27). He underscores that great outcomes are of no avail and in fact may be discredited if one's character flaws disqualify the leader in the end. To his critics he appeals to his character as a leader when he writes, "We have wronged no one, we have corrupted no one, we have taken advantage of no one" (2 Cor. 7:2).

Then, when citing the qualifications for leadership to his colleague Timothy, Paul bypasses outcomes and goes right to the character of the leader's life. The leader must be *"above reproach, husband of one wife, sober-minded, self-controlled, respectable, hospitable, able to teach, not a drunkard, not violent but gentle, not quarrelsome, not a lover of money ... managing his own household well with all dignity ... well thought of by outsiders"* (1 Tim. 3:2 – 7).

It is safe to say that Scripture never discounts character to celebrate the outcomes of a leader. In fact, I am still in the hunt to find a passage that affirms outcomes regardless of character. In God's economy the end does not justify the means. With him it's always about the means ... the process by which outcomes are achieved.

GETTING THE PROCESS RIGHT

I recall sitting on a beach with a retired aerospace executive who had become a consultant for quality control to several Forbes 500 companies. Being interested in quality control (an important part of what leaders do), I asked him to tell me about the principles that he used to guarantee the quality of the product. I was under the impression that quality control people stood at the end of the line, inspected the toaster, and if the toaster wasn't right, sent it back to get it fixed. To my surprise, the retired executive told me that quality control had nothing to do with the product and everything to do with the process. He said, "If the process is right, the product is guaranteed! Our sole focus is on process."

Character drives the process of successful leadership. When we process our leadership by our character, the quality of the outcomes will be measured by a thriving culture where people are valued and not used, where the leader is respected and not feared, where a leader is trusted and not doubted, where the moral authority of the leader's life makes others glad to cooperate and achieve, where grace underwrites the administration of the employee handbook, and where the leader's example stimulates those he serves to live and lead as the leader lives and leads. A leader who has chosen to lead by character motivates a community of followers who gladly embrace the mission of the enterprise and who are happily motivated to deliver quality outcomes.

THE TALE OF TWO KINGS

I have always been fascinated with the contrast between Israel's first two kings. Saul had all the outward trappings of a successful leader. As Scripture records, he was "a handsome young man. There was not a man among the people of Israel more handsome than he. From his shoulders upward he was taller than any of his people" (1 Sam. 9:2 – 3). Not only was he the poster boy for how leaders should look, but by all accounts he achieved some pretty spectacular outcomes.

Yet the narrative indicates that there was something wrong with how Saul processed his leadership. The "something wrong" begins to show up early in the story. After the amazing affirmation of being anointed as king by the lead prophet of the day, Samuel (1 Sam. 10:1 – 13), Saul is hesitant to tell his uncle that he has been anointed king (vv. 14 – 16). Moreover, when he is to be introduced to Israel as king, he is found hiding in the baggage.

While I am hesitant to psych out the text, it does seem that there are troubling insecurities deep inside of too tall Saul. Instead of believing in God's anointing and stepping up to the task with an appropriate sense of God-ordained confidence and unflinching surrender to God's authority, he manages his leadership by his natural instincts. Could it be that these instincts, driven by his insecurities, tempted Saul to use his leadership platform to prove something to himself about himself?

Before long, Saul is seen to be seeking ways to relieve his insecurities by affirming and elevating himself through military conquest, by building a self-honoring statue, by seeking self-serving advice and affirmation from heretical sources, by rationalizing his failures and lying his way out of trouble, by using his conquests for personal gain, and in the end by making himself miserable with anger toward those who threatened his position and power.

It is worthy of note that particularly in the beginning of his rule he had the appearance of godliness, spoke the Word of God, and indeed produced spectacular military outcomes. But clearly God was not impressed. In fact, the commentary on his leadership is both sobering and sad: "And the word of the Lord came to Samuel: I regret that I have made Saul King" (1 Sam. 15:10 – 11).

These are words that none of us want to hear from God in regard to our leadership!

So what is God looking for in a leader? Earlier in Saul's reign, Samuel warns him that God, displeased with Saul's leadership, has decided that his kingdom will not continue and that the Lord has "sought out a man after his own heart, and the Lord has commanded him to be prince over his people" (1 Sam. 13:14).

Enter David!

Rejecting the tall and strong likely leaders in Jesse's family, the selection arrow points to the youngest son, who is so unlikely that he is not even invited to the "let's choose a leader" event. Yet David, in spite of his seemingly unqualified résumé, was exactly the one God was looking for. The one whom God could trust with his people. Not only had David learned to lead confidently, given the presence and power of God in his life — have you ever licked a lion barehanded? — but he also developed the character quality of being a trusted servant to his family and their flock. It was in those quiet hours of shepherding that he drew close to God and cultivated a heart after God's own heart! He proved the point when, jealous for the reputation of the God of Israel, he risked his life against a taunting giant. He was just what God was looking for in a leader for his people.

Unlikely?

Unlikely to everyone but God. While David was not always exemplary — at times far from perfect — he was a leader who first and foremost had a heart after God's own heart. His heart for God was demonstrated even in his worst failures. Unlike Saul, his conscience was actively chasing him down (Ps. 32). And when confronted, he repented with a wrenching depth of sincerity (Ps. 51). No excuses, no rationalization. He was willing to admit how deeply flawed he was. His character drove his recovery. He was good on the inside.

Leaders who have a heart after God's heart, in the end, lead the way

God would lead. And, it should not go unnoticed that God himself leads from and through his character. All of his deliberations, decisions, and directives are driven by the richness of *who he is* at the core: just, loving, merciful, gracious, forgiving, serving, enduring, generous, tolerant, and so much more. You can count on him to consistently lead us by these character qualities. He cannot deny himself!

In addition, the act of replacing Saul with David demonstrates that from God's perspective, great and trusted leaders are those who have chosen to lead from the heart-side out. They are leaders after God's own heart. They lead with character as God leads with character.

CHAPTER 2

THE UNLIKELY LEADER

Dealing with the Delusions

Bob settled into his seat at the Pastor's Conference. He had been looking forward to being here for months. Just getting out of the church environment for five days seemed like a well-deserved reward in light of the stress of dealing with ministry challenges the other 360 days of the year. He had come alone, and that was fine with him. Solitude and being free to make his own decisions about how he would use his time were rare commodities. In his darker moments he had even thought that he wouldn't take notes or engage too seriously. He was just glad that he was out of the environment that often reminded him of how out of control leadership seems to be when you are working with people.

Maybe it would be here that he could forget how his dreams for becoming a great leader had long ago been swallowed up into the fog of ministry uncertainties. The banner that stretched over the platform read, "Relax, For Once You're Not In Charge."

"That," thought Bob, "is *exactly* what I like about being here!"

All was well.

At least until the nagging insecurities about his leadership abilities showed up ... again.

The keynote speaker for the opening evening had just walked in. He looked confident and upbeat as he gladly signed one of his books that an admiring fan had pushed toward him. And what was the speaker texting as he distractedly talked with admirers ... or was he tweeting to his extensive following? Bob wasn't jealous. In fact, he had always been blessed by the ministry of the high-profile leader. Bob simply felt that by comparison he was...

- inadequate
- unsuccessful
- unimportant
- unrecognized
- unappreciated
- undervalued
- not much of a leader
- way down the food chain
- in the end, unlikely to do much for God

The insecurities that had haunted him since seminary were now in high gear. He had read the book but didn't feel that he had ever moved from "Good to Great."[2] In his worst moments he wondered if he had even made it to "good." He felt insignificant and alone.

But he wasn't alone. There were others there that night thinking the same thing ... feeling the same way.

Not everyone, of course. Several of the attendees were just starting out in leadership roles. For them, the leader-speaker and his highly branded ministry represented a goal to attain. No doubt a few who were in the room that night would eventually find themselves climbing the ladder to apparent success. Some would make it happen by asserting themselves on upward trajectories of self-promotion. Others would get there because, like turtles on a fence post, God would put them there. Those in the self-promotion camp would likely struggle with pride, feeling that they have been responsible for their own success. Those placed by God would be humbly grateful — a bit surprised that they had ended up where they are.

---

2. As in the book *Good to Great: Why Some Companies Make the Leap ... and Others Don't* by Jim Collins (New York: HarperBusiness, 2001).

But what about those who won't make the assent? Because most won't. What if ten years from now they are still in the same seemingly insignificant ministry? Unrecognized and financially strapped. No entourage. No invitations to speak at conferences or to write best-selling books. No followers on Twitter. What will happen when they realize that they will never be successful by those standards? What will they do when their visions of sugar plums turn into sour grapes? What then? What of the discouragement and despair? What of the loss of self-confidence? What of the down-deep-inside desire to bail?

My guess would be that few if any of the attendees understood that the root of their aspirations and struggles was a debilitating focus on self.

SELF-CONSUMING DYNAMICS

Outcome-driven leaders ultimately suffer from self-consuming dynamics in times of both success and failure. When great outcomes are on a roll, self-reliance, self-adulation, and self-promotion dominate their souls. But when outcomes are not all they dreamed they would be and the enterprise seems to be going south, then self-pity, self-doubt, and a host of self-consuming insecurities deflate them at the core.

Character-driven leaders, by contrast, while not exempt from disappointment and seasons of difficulty, have ballast in their souls. They know that their leadership is not about self-advance, but about stewarding the environment where God has put them, for his glory and gain. In good times they are very much aware that if it weren't for the favor of God, the gifts he has given them, and the hard work of those around them, nothing good would have ever happened. They rejoice in giving credit to others and glory to God.

In tough times they remain undauntedly God-focused. They have cultivated the character to see trials and difficulties through the lens of God's work in and through their lives. They use difficulty to look for signs of productive reproof so that they might repent and lead more effectively in the future. They see difficulties as an opportunity to exemplify the character of Jesus in his suffering. They are unflinchingly linked to Christ and find their confidence in him. They are like the old punching dummies.

Anchored at the base with a solid weight when you punch them, they fall over, only to pop upright again.

Character-driven leaders are resilient because they are not self-consumed. Their leadership is not about them, but about Christ and his kingdom.

Of all the thoughts that Bob had while sitting in the crowd at the conference that night, he never considered that in the grand scheme of God's purposes he may have been exactly where God wanted him to be and may have actually been doing exactly what God wanted him to do as a leader. Or that God may actually be pleased with him. In fact, he may have had far more potential to be an effective leader in kingdom terms than the high profile speaker who was acclaimed and admired by the crowd. The truth is that we all, like Bob, live under a set of delusions about leadership.

We tend to be deluded about the significance of great outcomes, what outcomes say about the approval of God, and the role that size plays in the evaluation of successful leadership.

Delusion 1: Outcomes are the primary measure of success.

The more a person accomplishes, the better the chances are that they will be hailed as a great leader. Leadership books support this delusion by touting the priority of setting goals and objectives and then providing leaders with "ten" motivational tactics to get those who work for them to accomplish those goals with little or no reference to the importance of the character of a leader. It is easy for a leader to follow the advice and generate admirable outcomes ... with little thought of caring for who they are at the core, of how they have led, or of celebrating the minions in the hold of the ship who are pulling on the oars of the enterprise.

This "externals trump internals" delusion was underscored in an interesting exchange between a nationally applauded, high-profile pastor and Francis Chan. The founder of a highly visible ministry and a well-published author, Chan decided to step down from the church as lead pastor. Concerned about what his increasingly high profile, the busyness of traveling, writing, and conference speaking was doing to him inside his head and his heart, he resigned from his church and gave himself to ministering to the poor. This enabled him to create space in his life to measure and adjust his internal focus. To guard and cultivate who he should be on the inside. The interviewer, who seemed disconnected from the fact that there might be value in Chan's decision, queried Chan about how the church could go on without him at the helm. Chan replied that the elders were a gifted group and that the church would be in good shape in his absence.

Incredulous, the questioner went on to say, "But who will preach?"

Chan replied, "Our executive pastor."

"But is he good?" was the response.

In fairness to the interviewer, I'm sure that his intentions were well meaning. But in the interview it was clear that who you are and who you are becoming are not as important as your performance and your prominence as a leader. Under the surface of the questions there are a set of assumptions. These assumptions celebrate external outcomes over internal development. Assumptions such as, "There is little value in prioritizing who you are and or what kind of person you are becoming if it means you have to leave your highly leveraged position. Stay in the limelight and continue to believe that your church cannot make it without you! You are the leader, and your presence is the most important thing in your church." Or, "Churches need someone who is 'good' in the pulpit in order to be effective and to maintain their trajectory."

Obviously, no one wants a bad preacher in the pulpit, and it is important to think through the impact of a high-profile leader stepping out of the limelight. But it is significant that in the interview, Chan's decision to value his personhood and to be concerned about what he was becoming was never affirmed … just challenged. Chan's work in building into the people around him so that the church would be able to succeed without him was never applauded … just ignored. And what if the executive pastor was not a "good" preacher? What if the best messages he preached were the messages from his life … from who he is and how he leads? What if the flock's growth was accelerated by B+ sermons from a "life-well-lived" leader?

This "externals trumps internals" delusion seemed evident as well when I listened to a discussion on the importance of being authentic. In my mind, authenticity is one of the character qualities of effective leadership, so the topic drew me in. To my surprise, the conversation centered on the thought that authenticity is simply being who you are and expecting that others will accept you that way.

That seemed strange to me. As a follower of Christ, I have always thought that authenticity means living up to who I claim to be in Christ. Which means that I am not satisfied with who I am in the raw. Living up to who I claim to be in Christ requires that I desire to change, to humbly repent, to admit my faults and failures, and to be open to have my life sharpened by others who live more consistently like Jesus than I do.

When leaders think that in the end people need to simply accept them as they are, character deficiencies and all, then "how" they do ministry and "who they are" as they do ministry will likely not come into play.

So here is the head-scratcher. Does anyone seem to care about the internal dynamics of leadership? It concerned me to hear a congregant say about their pastor, "I don't want to know what kind of a person he is. I just love sitting under his ministry."

But ...

- What if character precedes competency?
- What if integrity has been eclipsed by a pragmatic interest in outcomes?
- What if people serve the leader for reasons other than an admiration of the leader as a person and a soul-mate companionship on the journey with the leader?
- What if it's possible to have impressive short-term results but long-term downsides that in the end discredit those outcomes?
- What if someone who is not in the limelight might be able, through their character and the way they lead, to have outcomes that in the long run are more lasting and God honoring?
- What if leaving a significant legacy is not measured by what we accomplish today, but by the impact of a life well lived over the long term or even beyond our lifetime in the lives of others?

Delusion 2: Great outcomes affirm God's approval.

It's easy to assume that high-output leaders have the approval of God on their lives and leadership. After all, if God wasn't pleased with them, he wouldn't bless them with success. So God's work through them validates their life and leadership. Hence, the leader should be given a hall pass on behavior and style because seemingly God is okay with doing great things through them.

More serious than this faulted perception that others may have about leaders is that leaders themselves can be tempted to feel that the way they lead and who they are as they lead is affirmed by the fact that God is using them. Which means, if the outcomes are in place, then they can be comfortable with who they are, regardless of the faults and flaws.

I recall talking with a highly acclaimed leader about an aspect of his life that had come into question. He dismissed my concern by responding that his ministry and preaching had never been more effective. He was under the delusion that God's positive work through him affirmed that God was pleased with him and his life.

Actually, it's possible that his success may have had little to do with God's approval, but rather was a reflection of God's amazing patience and his unending passion to bless his people in spite of the leader's behavior.

I doubt if anyone will argue that Moses stands as a stellar example of leadership in terms of both character and outcomes. As Scripture points out, he was meek, willing to take counsel, a passionate advocate for God's mercy on those who were rebellious and disobedient, and jealous for God's reputation through his leadership, and as such ranks as one of the few in Scripture who have the honor of being called a "friend of God." And, through his surrendered character, God chose to produce amazing outcomes. Just think of what God did through him as he out-performed Egypt's best magicians in front of Pharaoh, and what about the amazing Red Sea experience, to say nothing of moving masses of grumpy people toward the Promise Land?

But as stellar as Moses' character and outcomes were, one moment in his leadership history demonstrates that dramatic outcomes are never a sign that God endorses the way we lead or who we are as we lead. In fact, it demonstrates that God will hold the leader, even the best of us, accountable in spite of the outcomes.

In summer 2012, Martie and I trekked through the Sinai desert in 115-degree weather. It was evident that the essential ingredient for comfort, let alone survival, was water. It gave us an upfront and personal realization of what it meant for the wandering people of Israel to be in need of water — and why they would complain if there was no liquid refreshment in sight.

Wanting to meet the needs of his parched people, God instructed Moses to speak to the rock as a means of releasing God's power to make clear, cool water flow to satisfy their thirst. Moses, clearly annoyed by the murmuring masses, gathered the people and in anger struck the rock … twice! In the process he shouted, "Must *we* give you water from this rock?" As Numbers records,

> Then Moses and Aaron gathered the assembly together before the rock, and he said to them, "Hear now, you rebels: shall we bring water for you out of this rock?" And Moses lifted up his hand and struck the rock with his staff twice, and water came out abundantly, and the congregation drank and their livestock (Num. 20:10).

Clearly, in that instance God produced amazing outcomes through Moses on behalf of his people. But while God was willing to use Moses to bless his people, he clearly was not pleased with Moses. Immediately on the heels of Moses' success God responded to the incident, "Because you did not … uphold me as holy in the eyes of the people of Israel, therefore you shall not bring this assembly into the land that I have given them" (Num. 20:12).

Moses' striking the rock in anger and claiming that he and Aaron would bring them water from the rock was an offense to the holiness of God. God was intent on mercifully loving his murmuring people with the miracle of water from a rock. Moses' anger graffitied the face of a loving God at the "water event." And taking the credit by claiming that he and Aaron would give them water from the rock robbed God of his glory. As the Psalmist says, "He sinned with his lips" (Ps. 106:33).

I wonder if this is what Paul had in mind when he said that he disciplined his life, "lest after preaching to others I myself should be disqualified" (1 Cor. 9:27).

God is *always* concerned about how we do what we do. And he cares deeply about who we are as we do what we do. God loved his people and wanted to bless them with water, so he was willing to use a disobedient leader to do it. Then, after the people were blessed, he took Moses to the woodshed. Anyone given the right gifts and opportunities can produce outcomes … even jaw-dropping ones. And, God is willing to bless his people even through high-outcome, disobedient leaders. But we wrongly assume that those outcomes are a stamp of God's approval on the leader's life or style.

It's worthy of note that Aaron, who said nothing and did nothing, was held accountable as well. Which may have something to say to those who support and enable leaders in lifestyles and leadership styles that are inconsistent with God's holy and righteous ways.

Delusion 3: The size of the enterprise validates the success of the leader.

Recently I was being interviewed over lunch by a denominational leader about leadership and its place and importance in ministry. The conversation followed all the usual rabbit trails of the ins and outs of leadership. But it was his last question about leadership that gave me pause.

"Who do you admire as a leader?"

My hesitation must have been a surprise to him. I began thinking about the leaders I personally know. Initially, everyone on my first list was highly "successful." They all had broad name recognition and had built sizable enterprises. But as I thought it through, I wasn't sure that some of them were admirable in terms of being known for their outstanding character. My mind then shifted to other leaders who were off the radar in terms of being a highly acclaimed leader. These are leaders whom I have known and watched, who, though unknown and unlikely, were leading with strong character in ways that glorified God and blessed the flock.

This past Easter, Martie and I attended a small church in rural Michigan. The pastor has served there for the last eighteen years. I watched the pastor relate to the people and marveled at the connectivity, love, and pastoral concern that he demonstrated. According to friends who attend his church, his life and loving leadership of the flock has given him not only a platform of influence with his people but also a place of influence in the community at large. His leadership style makes Jesus and Christianity an attractive reality.

Leaders like this inspire me. I admire them. With little or no recognition, they bloom for Jesus where they are planted. I am confident their outcomes will be some of heaven's great stories.

A colleague of mine accepted a position in a city where the nearest neighborhood church was a small congregation located in a culturally diverse area. He and his wife felt strongly that they should attend a church that was geographically closest to them. This decision led to some definite culture shock for them. They were used to attending large churches where the preaching was captivating and those around them looked like them and shared the same values they held. Their new church was quite different. It was composed of different kinds of people representing a broad array of nationalities and, quite literally, the lame, the outcast, and the socially marginalized.

The pastor had been there for many years, and in spite of the fact that his preaching was well below normal standards, he noted that his people admired and respected him. My colleague told me that it was this pastor's character that won his admiration. In fact, the pastor modeled several traits my colleague desired to cultivate in his own life.

While many leaders look good from a distance, it's possible that getting close can be a disappointment. With this pastor, the closer you got to him, the better he looked. My colleague told me that one evening he was at a neighborhood get-together in the guild hall. He noticed that when the pastor and his wife walked in, the people in the room lit up. After years of his investing seeds of love and care into the neighborhood, the community had grown to admire their local minister. In a tough, street-wise, urban neighborhood ... character wins! And it was the character of that unlikely leader that created a platform for the gospel to thrive in an unlikely place.

I sometimes think about the great "awards assembly" we will have one day in heaven. The Bible tells us that there will come a day when Jesus will publicly recognize those who have served him faithfully (1 Cor. 3:10 – 15). Though I might like to imagine myself sitting in the front row with my name at the top of the program, the truth is that the greatest rewards will likely be for those who have labored in obscurity, men and women you have never heard about. As Francis Schaeffer once wrote: "... with God there are no small people and no small places." Those who faithfully lead with character in the "small" places — the unlikely, unnoticed leaders — may not gain acclaim in this life, but great will be their reward in heaven.

Yet, sometimes the thought that unlikely, unnoticed leaders can be highly effective in small places gets lost in our "bigger is better" world.

IS BIGGER BETTER?

In an interview in the United Kingdom, a stateside megachurch pastor queried the interviewee about the dearth of famous Bible-teachers and megachurches in England. His comments seemed to suggest that the lack of high-profile preachers and large regional churches meant there was something wrong with Christianity in that country.

That assumption lacks an awareness of what's really "big" with God.

All over the world there are unlikely character-driven leaders who serve in small yet significant ways. Many of them are persecuted and meet underground at the risk of their lives. Others gather in clearings in the jungle and in apartments in bustling cities with the shades drawn. These are leaders who understand the meaning of the words *sacrifice* and *suffering*. They pick up their cross and lead with pure motives and rich character, embracing Jesus as the model for how they lead. For them, "size" is never a consideration.

Nor has "big churches and notable Bible teachers" ever been a standard for effectiveness in places like China, where — after all the missionaries were martyred or expelled in the 1940s — the headcount of Christians grew exponentially, with no megachurches and no nationally known Bible teachers. When the missionaries left, there were estimated to be about one million Christians in China. Now, by even conservative accounts, there are nearly 100 million followers of Jesus. Moreover, this marginalized, persecuted church has birthed a generation that is determined that they will take the gospel back to Jerusalem on the Silk Road trade routes, through hostile Muslim territory. It is a generation that says, "Who is better to take the gospel to hostile people? We know how to suffer, how to be imprisoned, how to go hungry, and how to face death for Christ."

I will lead the cheering section for them any day!

When I was serving at the Moody Bible Institute in Chicago, we had a handful of students from the underground church in China. I recall talking with them on one occasion and wondering out loud if the fact that they have graduated from Moody would give them credibility when they went home to serve the church in China. To my surprise, they quickly disregarded my rather self-serving thought and said, "When we go home, the elders will listen to us pray. That is what will give us credibility." I walked away knowing that the church in China had propelled its kingdom work, not by highly credentialed leaders, but by intimacy with Jesus on bended knee. I was impressed and convicted.

My point in all of this is not to suggest that larger churches cannot be used by God. Certainly God uses large churches and well-known leaders to advance his cause, and the vast majority of them lead with godly lives. For this, I am incredibly thankful. But we must never forget that God does not value them more than those who lead in less recognizable contexts. In fact, in some of those out-of-the-way places and through the lives of many of those unlikely leaders, God is doing great things over the long term ultimately with exponential results.

The most influential man in my own life grew up in a small farming village in southern Michigan. He was led to the Lord by Pastor White, the long-term pastor of First Baptist Church in the sparsely populated village of Colon. Pastor White mentored and encouraged him to leave the farm to attend Wheaton College. This young, college-bound freshman so admired the quality and caliber of Pastor White's life and ministry that he left the farm with a desire to become a pastor just like his pastor.

The Lord catapulted the life and ministry of Pastor White's understudy, and he eventually became the pastor of an influential church on the outskirts of New York City. As a result of his faithful service at First Baptist Church in Hackensack, New Jersey, many young people went to the mission field, and others gave their lives to serve the Lord in a variety of ministries. This young man influenced top-level Manhattan executives, helping them to see their high-profile positions as opportunities to magnify Christ and advance his purpose. He impacted the global cause of Christ by serving on mission boards and the board of a leading seminary.

The boy that Pastor White mentored was my dad.

The thing I remember most about my father, more than all of his great accomplishments as a pastor, was his character. He was a man of integrity and godliness. Famous Bible teachers and preachers would tell me that they admired my dad and that I was blessed to have him as a father. And I agreed. I was always proud to be known as the son of Joseph Stowell. And, I am involved today in kingdom leadership because of my dad's influence on my life.

All that God has done through my dad's life, through the opportunities I have had to serve and lead, and all that he is doing through my sons and daughter who are all actively engaged in fruitful ministry . . . it can all be traced back and directly attributed to Pastor White, an unlikely leader who with magnetic character faithfully labored where God had placed him. Content in his calling, he faithfully carried out his work as shepherd of the flock with a depth of character that indelibly impressed one young man under his care.

Count on it: Even though he wrote no books, had no media ministry, and probably had an outdated church logo, Pastor White was a smashing success in God's eyes. One day I will thank him personally for investing in my father, a man who inspired me with a joy-filled vision of serving the Lord in ministry.

I find it interesting that churches, ministries, and organizations that are built to great proportions often have a shelf life. I could generate a long list of "great" churches that are now in decline. Pastor White never built a great church. He built great people by modeling a life well lived. I will be forever grateful that my Dad was one of them!

Come to think of it . . . Jesus never built a great church. He built into twelve men who then did great things for the kingdom. They were twelve men who maximized outcomes for Christ long after Jesus ascended. Could it be that God has put you in a seemingly insignificant place with not many spectacular results because he wants you to influence some young person in your church with your character-driven leadership who will then in their generation do expansive things for God long after you are gone?

It's not that all character-driven leaders will have smaller, unheralded spheres of influence. Nor is there something wrong with those who are called to build churches and organizations that have massive boundaries and global influence. Character-driven maximum leadership in the end is not about what you have built — big or not so big. It is about who you are as you build, and how you have chosen to generate your outcomes. And with that matrix of success in mind, even those who don't achieve worldly notoriety can in effect be wonderfully successful in God's eyes.

Bloom where you are planted!

Each summer Martie and I spend a week with our children, their spouses, and our grandchildren at a lake in northern Michigan. We schedule a lot of fun things throughout the week, including late-night fireworks on the beach. Few things have more "wow" power than lighting up the sky for wide-eyed kids. But the wow outcomes of our programming for the week mean nothing if over the course of the year Martie and I don't take time to love our grandchildren and build into their lives. The results of loving and building into their lives are not always immediately spectacular, sometimes are not immediately rewarding, and usually do not engender much applause. However, in the long run it is far more significant than the fireworks.

Character-driven leadership runs by the same dynamics.

Bob had never thought of effective leadership as being more about how he leads and who he is as he leads than about producing noticeable outcomes. It had never crossed his mind that leading from a godly, authentic, and perseveringly faithful life for Jesus might have such a phenomenal impact on the life of a boy or girl in his church that in their lifetime they would be exponentially used by God. Or that long after he was gone, he would have influenced and motivated someone to be an impactful evangelist, author, corporate leader, teacher, or artist whose influence for Christ would far exceed the outcomes of Bob's life or the size of the ministry that he built.

It had not crossed his mind that character-driven, maximum leadership did not revolve around his visibility as a highly acclaimed leader, but that the measure of his leadership would be what happens in the lives of people … in the long term … because of how he led and the character he displayed as he led. Perhaps it would be evident in the lives of his own children as they blossom in their generation because their dad's life at home and in private was not different from what he preached in the pulpit.

Ultimately, all of us who are called to lead will make a choice about what kind of leader we will be. An outcome-driven leader whose glory is in the organizational outcomes, or a character-driven leader whose approach to leadership is an unlikely, counterintuitive radically different pattern of influence? The choice will determine two radically different styles and two radically different outcomes. Jesus speaks to these styles and outcomes in two poignant passages.

CHAPTER 3

TAKING LEADERSHIP PERSONALLY

The How and Who of Leadership

Ken is a second-generation CEO of a globally successful company. He grew up in a Christian home and often eavesdropped on theological discussions between his dad and dinner guests in their dining room after church on Sundays. Under his dad's leadership the company was highly successful. His family lived in the best house in the neighborhood, and the family name was highly regarded in the community. His father's business prowess and entrepreneurial instincts were widely heralded.

Ken started working in his dad's business when he was twelve years old. As the years progressed, he sensed a major disconnect between what he heard from his dad during his after-dinner theological discussions on Sundays and the way the business was run. Ken worked on the line with poor, underpaid workers and heard chatter on the production floor about how poorly people were treated and how those who ran the company had little regard for anything but the bottom line. The working environment focused on one outcome: making Ken's dad a success. The people who worked there were a means to an end.

Today Ken runs the company. But he runs it differently than his father. His management style is directed and motivated by his commitment to lead as a follower of Jesus and to bring the values of the Kingdom to bear on the enterprise. When the economy forced him to downsize, he gave the employees a year's notice and initiated a program to retrain and replace those who were losing their jobs. All of the displaced workers who wanted another job were placed elsewhere. At the company, immigrant workers can take English classes on company time and at company expense. Ken's goal, as a business owner, is to enable and empower underprivileged employees to develop skills and language proficiency. The turnover rate at his company has decreased by 200 percent. People love working for Ken. And the company has grown significantly.

Ken's commitment to live and lead as a follower of Jesus has spilled over into community leadership as well. Through a coalition of companies he helps provide job training and placement effort, which include helping people with felonies in their past find jobs, providing transportation for poor workers to their workplace, and several other initiatives that enrich lives. The mission statement of his massively successful enterprise has little to do with corporate outcomes. It is simple and to the point: "To Enrich Lives."

Ken and his dad both produced significant corporate outcomes. They both led a successful business. But Ken's approach to leadership focuses on more than the corporate bottom line. Beyond the fact that his company supplies butter all over the world, Ken is acutely aware of the fact that *how* he leads reflects *who* he is as he leads and is core to leadership success. Ken is not content to use people to build a thriving enterprise. Instead, as a Christ follower he identifies himself as a servant of others and uses his business not just to achieve personal profits, but to build great people.

Yes, Ken drives a nice car, lives in a great house, and will sometimes stay at high end resorts. But years from now, his wealth will not be his legacy. Soon, the money he has accumulated will be forgotten and there will be other, far more successful corporate executives and noteworthy companies. Ken's legacy will be generational, the product of his relationships with others and the time and investment he has made into their lives. His influence will be etched in the lives of the workers he has trained, cared for, and empowered to advance their own lives in significant ways. Men and women who work for him have been inspired by his passion and commitment to serve them and will raise families where children grow up believing that they can do good for others as well. Ken's legacy, for generations to come, will be told in the lives that he has enriched and blessed.

Ken would be one of the first to tell you that he is an unlikely leader. He is not very aggressive. He easily blends into the crowd. But he has thought deeply about *how* he wants to lead. And he knows *who* he is in Christ as he leads.

If you want your leadership to have lasting generational impact, you need to think about *how* you will lead and *whom* you will be like as you lead.

HOW WE LEAD

Jesus told an interesting story about building — which is a great metaphor about leadership, since leaders build. It's the story of two builders who each built a house for themselves (Matt. 7:24 – 27). To the casual observer, the builder who finished his home first would be considered more successful, since he built his house more quickly. We might imagine him sitting by the pool and sipping a cool drink while the other builder is still laboring to fulfill his dream. The builder by the pool wins, and the one with his shovel still in the ground is the loser.

But Jesus takes us beyond the moment to the end game. He concludes that the slower builder who cared about how he built was, in fact, the wise builder. The clever, fast-tracked builder was in the end foolish and his legacy devastated by the fragile superstructure that he erected. The difference, according to Jesus, was not in what they built, but in how they built. The clear implication is that buildings that last are built on foundations that are more difficult to establish and are more painstakingly accomplished.

Yet, more significant in terms of leadership, according to the story, the wise builder builds according to the specifications of the words and ways of Jesus. In the words of Jesus, "Everyone then who hears these words of mine and does them will be like a wise man who built his house on the rock" (Matt. 7:24).

The story about the two builders is the concluding punch to the now famous Sermon on the Mount, in which Jesus has in effect laid out the ways and wisdom of the kingdom. In essence, it is the constitution of his kingdom. Contradictory to conventional wisdom and amazingly counter-intuitive, it is clear from this sermon that the kingdom of heaven runs on a far different set of principles and practices than the kingdoms of the fallen world in which we live. According to the sermon, the kingdom of Christ is about the value of being poor in spirit, meek, and merciful; mourning, hungering, and thirsting for righteousness; turning the other cheek and being quick to forgive, being generous, loving enemies, caring for the poor; and a bundle of other upside-down thoughts about life and leadership. The catch: These are all values that are difficult to cultivate and challenging to apply.

Building on this radically different, more-difficult-to-achieve foundation gives me pause about most of the leadership books that I have read and some of the leadership advice that I have been given. "Successful" leaders are anything but meek, merciful, and poor in spirit. Meekness would be a liability in most leadership profiles. The poverty of spirit that recognizes how fallen, frail, and faulted we are at the core is out. Instead, self-confidence is the game changer. Powerful leaders control the environment by getting angry, punishing those who step out of bounds, and demanding repentance and remediation to those who have wronged them. Mercy and turning the other cheek are a liability.

"Successful" leaders outdistance their competitors and take them down when they can. They lead to gain for themselves instead of leading to give it away. They bask in the limelight.

In the end, it seems as if most leadership principles that are paraded out for hope-to-be successful Christian leaders are not much different than the leadership books written for secular leaders. Advice from business entrepreneurs such as Jack Welch and Bill Gates often commands more attention and applause than the leadership wisdom of Jesus.

None of us are immune to the temptation to lead by our own instincts. And, quite frankly, we don't need a lot of advice about leading in counter-kingdom ways. Much of the wrongness of our leading ... much of the shallowness of our foundations ..., as we have learned, comes naturally.

So Jesus gives us non-negotiable principles for how we lead in his sermon that by now is more famous than followed. While we preach the principles of the sermon to our people, we need to remember that kingdom leaders don't get an exemption on the building specifications that Jesus gives us in the Sermon on the Mount. If the kingdom of Christ is not of this world, then it seems a great contradiction for kingdom of Christ leaders to be leading by advice and values that are of this world. It's not that all secular advice for leaders is wrong. I would just want to vet it all by the words and ways of Jesus so that in the end, the house that I've built will stand.

Christ told the story of the two builders to make the point that *how you build* is of utmost importance. It's no wonder, then, that Paul, using the same building metaphor, warns leaders to be careful *how* they build, lest their building be nothing more than "wood, hay, stubble" burned to a pile of ashes in the end (see 1 Corinthians 3:10 – 15 KJV). As Francis Schaeffer once quipped, none of us wants to be standing knee deep in a heap of ashes on that day. Or to put it another way, I doubt if any of us wants to be "ash-heap leaders"!

Character-driven leaders are committed to building their enterprise with the ways of Jesus as the guiding light of their leadership competency.

But it's not just *how* we lead that is important to Jesus. Into the tension of would-be leaders who were striving for position and power, Jesus raised the issue of the importance of *who we are* as we lead.

WHO WE ARE AS WE LEAD

I'm reminded of the intriguing moment in the lives of the disciples when James and John bring their mother to Jesus to see if she might be able to leverage their dreams to become the most important leaders in the kingdom (Matt. 20). She approaches Christ and asks if her two sons may sit the one on his right and the other on his left when he comes into the kingdom. In a monarchy, the ones who sit on each side of the king are the ones who have the seats of power and authority. It's clear that they want to be the most important persons in the new world order. And they weren't alone. The disciples were often debating about who would be the greatest in the kingdom.

So it's no wonder that Matthew admits that he and all the other would-be leaders were angry that James and John had asked for the positions of power and influence. The brothers had beaten the rest of them to the punch and, worse yet, had brought their mother to close the deal. As an aside, I have often reflected on the fact that some of the most committed individuals — those closest to Jesus — still had this "I-want-to-be-on-top" demon at work in their hearts. If they were driven by this leadership urge, then I don't think I'm exempt from the same self-promotional instincts.

So what will Jesus do?

He has selected a group of would-be leaders to carry the message and agenda of the kingdom to the known world. But it's all at risk now, because they have descended into the ditch of an all-out food fight for who will be the most important, the most powerful, the most highly recognized, and the most highly empowered leader in the kingdom. The clear danger here is that it is no longer about the kingdom agenda. It is now all about them and their desire for greatness.

If Jesus had been tuned in to current management philosophy, he may have told them to wait until everyone had taken the DISC test to see who was best qualified or said that the kingdom would be managed by teams where everyone had equal input.

But Jesus skips the management theory and queries them about who they are at the core. He says, "Are you able to drink the cup that I am to drink?" (Matt. 20:22). Referring to the suffering to come, he probes their courage and conviction quotients as first-step character traits for leading in his kingdom. No doubt, not knowing the extent of what he is asking, they affirm that they have what it takes.

Jesus then proceeds to tell them that high-profile leadership posts in the kingdom are not grabbed for, but are given by the Father. As he said, "To sit on my right hand and at my left is not mine to grant, but it is for those for whom it has been prepared by my Father" (v. 23). While it is important to have a deep desire to do great things for Christ and his kingdom, seeking to accomplish that by a self-asserting ascension to high-profile positions is against the grain of Jesus' way.

Those who land in high-profile positions should look back with a sense of surprise that they are there! There is a comfort and strength in knowing that God has managed your journey to a large sphere of leadership influence. It stimulates humility and gratitude and increases the sense of stewardship and accountability. When we grasp for leadership and self-promote our way to the top, it stimulates pride and a self-focused sense of ownership. It drives the leader to feel as if others owe him for his good work in building a large enterprise ... that he should be affirmed and applauded.

Grasping for and manipulating ourselves to the top is a dangerous pursuit.

When we are surprised by where we end up, we know that we owe God the glory and affirmation for advancing our frail and fallen selves into larger spheres of influence.

Having informed them that places of power are not grasped for but given by the Father, Jesus then, in typical fashion, radicalized the moment by articulating a clear contrast between who leaders think they are in the lower kingdom called "earth" and who they are to be as they lead in the kingdom of heaven. To contrast the opposing leadership styles, he said, "You know that the rulers of the Gentiles lord it over them, and their great ones exercise authority over them. It shall not be so among you. But whoever would be great among you must be your servant, and whoever would be first among you must be your slave" (Matt. 20:25 – 27).

Note the shift in emphasis. They were grasping for position, power, and applause — and Jesus stopped that instinct dead in its tracks and turned their heads and hearts to the counterintuitive kingdom dynamic. According to Jesus, leadership is not about the position that you hold or the power you get to leverage from that position. It's about who you are at the core and how you perceive yourself as a leader. Servanthood is a character trait. Servants know who they are, and that self-awareness determines how they act ... how they lead. Great outcomes follow.

Having been called to lead at Cornerstone University, I am aware of how imperative it is to remind myself that I am first and foremost a servant. I am not there to advance myself or to use the university to catapult me to fame, gain, or glory. Rather, I am to lead from my identity as a servant. I am there to serve the mission of the school and to give myself to advancing the best interests of the students, staff, and faculty. As a servant, I am not there to make myself great and not even there to make a great university to my glory, but to use my gifts and the resources of the school to make great people who will be impassioned and equipped to influence the cultures of our world for Christ.

When I am tempted to forget who I am as I lead, my mind reflects on the closing comments of Jesus as he wrapped up the "who-is-the-greatest-in-the-kingdom" controversy. For any of us who think we deserve to be more than a mere servant as we lead, Jesus reminds us that he himself came, not to be served, but to serve all the way to the cross, "to give his life as a ransom for many" (Matt. 20:28).

I have learned a lot of theological truths and have grown accustomed to the majesty and mystery of many of them. But I will never grow accustomed to the fact that when the Creator of the limitless universe and all the micro miracles of the invisible biological realms came to our earth, he chose to lead as a servant. Think of it: a Creator *Servant* King! And if he chose to use his position and power for the good and gain of others at the expense of himself, how much more should we be willing to recognize that who we are is a critical success factor in how we lead.

For those desiring to be character-driven leaders, Jesus matters! As such, his example guides our instincts toward true kingdom success.

As Paul instructs us,

> Have this mind among yourselves, which is yours in Christ Jesus, who, though he was in the form of God, did not count equality with God a thing to be grasped, but made himself nothing, taking the form of a servant, being born in the likeness of men. And being found in human form, he humbled himself by becoming obedient to the point of death, even death on a cross. Therefore God has highly exalted him and bestowed on him the name that is above every name, so that at the name of Jesus every knee should bow, in heaven and on earth and under the earth, and every tongue confess that Jesus Christ is Lord, to the glory of God the Father (Phil. 2:5 – 11).

Having this "mind" as a leader is no small thing! It is a huge step toward developing the character that needs to drive and define us as successful leaders. Kingdom leadership starts with leading in uncompromised obedience to the foundational counterintuitive ways of his Word and by knowing that we lead first as servants of Christ and as servants to those who are entrusted to our care.

The process of building our enterprise by the "hows" of Jesus and by adopting "who" we are as servants will face the challenge of the reality that much of this style of leadership goes against the grain of our own instinctive impulses. So what will be the motivating influence in our lives that leads us to live beyond our fallen selves and propels us to succeed as kingdom leaders?

As we will see in the chapters to come, Jesus offers us a new and radically different sense of identity that rescues us from our own muddled ways. This liberating perspective releases us to lead in ways that will produce broad and lasting influence for the glory of God and the good of others.

PART 2

A REDEFINED IDENTITY

Transformational Perspectives

CHAPTER 4

FOLLOWERSHIP

Following "the" Leader

I grew up as a PK (Preachers Kid). People in my dad's church expected that I would live up to that identity and behave as the local poster child for church etiquette. But it rarely worked out like that. In fact, I would love to have a five-dollar bill for every time someone said to me, "Young man — [I always knew I was in trouble when they started like that] — you should be an example! You are the pastor's son."

I didn't want to be an example … I was only five. But the point they were making was that if they could get me to think differently about who I was, it would transform the way I behaved.

Who we think we are drives and defines how we live and how we lead. If you think you are first and foremost a "leader," then you will act like a "leader." You will be aware that you are supposed to be in charge and that people should do what you tell them to do. You will be proud of your achievements and expect the praise and recognition you think you deserve. You will expect the best office in the building. You will feel entitled to the perks of being on top. You will expect to be highly compensated and to be treated as well as other leaders who lead similar organizations.

Leaders who self-identify as leaders get annoyed when people don't treat them as such. Annoyed when people criticize and don't honor them with respect. Annoyed when others don't agree with them and don't think their ideas are brilliant. Annoyed when they don't get the credit for the success of the organization. Annoyed when someone down the food chain seems to be more popular than they are.

But what if character-driven leaders don't think of themselves as leaders? What if they have a different sense of identity — a Christ-driven identity? An identity that transforms how they lead and who they are as they lead! An identity that enables them to become maximum leaders who lead according to the countercultural ways of the kingdom?

THE ALTERNATE IDENTITY

When I came to serve at Cornerstone University, one of the major brandings of the institution was its commitment to make leaders out of its students. The freshman discipleship experience was called "Leadership Journey," and all the focus of student development was on the production of successful leaders. I have no quarrel with the thought that our world is in desperate need of good leaders. So, on the surface it all seemed like a good idea — to say nothing of the fact that it was a great recruitment tool.

But in spite of the seeming rightness of the program, I feared that at the core it was fundamentally flawed. Flawed in the sense that if you are talking about positional leadership, then what of the majority of students who are not gifted to be leaders and who if forced into leadership positions would be frustrated and fail? Where does non-leader giftedness fit in a program built to produce leaders?

Thankfully, as I studied the program, it became evident that by leadership they really intended to focus on the leadership of personal influence. This would be a net wide enough to catch everyone, because we all can lead in terms of having a positive influence on our relationships, community, and culture regardless of our gifting.

But as good as this was, I felt there was still something missing. The missing ingredient was the essential navigational tool that should guide and advise all of life, especially the lives of those of us who are called to lead. This navigational tool — the GPS of leadership — is an identity that not only transforms all of life, but also transforms how we lead and who we are as we lead. Effective, character-driven leaders choose to identify themselves, first and foremost, as followers! Followers of Jesus. Only when we have a firm grasp of our identity as a follower of Jesus are we equipped to effectively lead and influence others.

LEADERSHIP REDEFINED

As soon as we began to articulate this fundamental principle of leadership on campus, it radically changed the program. You can imagine my delight when students began wearing T-shirts that boldly proclaimed, "Followership: leadership redefined!" I knew in my heart that if our students could learn to embrace the transformational identity of a follower, we stood a good chance of producing effective leaders. As long as I have a say in the matter, our university is committed to cultivating creative, intellectually capable, professionally adept followers of Jesus. We are convinced that if our students learn to see themselves this way, they will go on to distinguish themselves in their callings and careers and become effective influencers — maximum leaders — in our world for Christ. If I read Jesus right, raising up great leaders begins by teaching them to follow.

We have all seen leaders fail — morally, relationally, ethically, attitudinally, greedily, and from a host of different leadership traps. We've seen some fail as victims of burnout, derailed by disillusionment, and damaged by broken expectations. So the question remains: Why do leaders fail? I have rarely seen a leader fail because they are not gifted to lead. Most often a leader fails because at some point he or she has ceased to live and lead as a follower of Christ. Leaders take the first steps toward failure when they begin to assume that they are smart enough or skilled enough to succeed at what they do on their own. Guided by their own instincts and tempted by seductive opportunities, they turn their backs on Jesus, compromise their integrity, and are taken down by the belief that they are above the rules. Or they believe the lie that they are clever enough to avoid getting caught.

Leading by following insulates all of us from these kinds of failures. As long as we lead surrendered to the will, ways, and wisdom of Jesus, becoming an effective leader is well within our grasp. When Jesus began his mission by recruiting a group of men to be leaders in a global revolution that would change all of Western history, the first thing he said to them was, "Follow me!"

That invitation is still the first and fundamental calling of those who seek to lead toward maximum outcomes through the filter of Christ-like character.

FOLLOWERSHIP: STEP ONE IN LEADERSHIP!

Choosing the transformational identity of a "follower" as step one in the process of becoming a maximum leader is, like everything else in the kingdom, counterintuitive. Followers are the drones ... the minions ... the slaves in the mine ... the people who serve, who in the end make the leader successful. But Jesus turns the definitions of this world on their head and asserts that the way the world thinks has it wrong and that he has the corner on what is true and right.

This is the deal-breaker moment in this book. The question is, "Are you ready to accept the identity of a follower ... to fully surrender to Jesus as the final authority on life and leading?"

Are you ready to have him challenge you in the arenas of who you are and how you lead? Will you let him unfetter you from the delusions of leadership according to the world's way? Will you let him challenge your misperception that because something works, it must be right and good? And will you let him re-work you in the areas of self, ambition, authority, power, and expectations? If you are not open to this kind of personal radicalization that Jesus has in mind for you, then you will most likely find the rest of this book annoying.

But if you are willing to hear his call to follow him, if you agree to choose the identity that he calls you to — that is, to no longer think of yourself as a leader but to take step one toward maximum leadership by accepting the adventuresome, challenging, and sometimes troubling honor of following him — then let's talk about the difference that following Jesus makes in a leader's life.

THREE TRANSFORMING DYNAMICS IN THE LIFE OF A FOLLOWER

There are three dynamics of followership that transform a leader from instinctive outcome-driven leadership to character-driven leadership. One has to do with the cultural context into which Jesus spoke his call for early disciples to become followers. The other two flow out of the meaning of the word *follow* as Matthew used it in his gospel (see 4:18 – 22).

Dynamic #1: Follower-leaders count it an honor to follow Jesus.

For those of us who see a commitment to following Jesus as another task on the list of Christian things successful leaders must do, we need to think again! It is not a task; it is a compelling honor!

When Jesus called his disciples to follow him, it wasn't just a random invitation. These soon-to-be leaders of the early church knew exactly what he meant. For them, becoming a follower of a rabbi was a highly honored privilege, something beyond the reach of most Jewish men.

Jewish boys began attending rabbi school at the age of about five and continued their learning under the rabbi's tutelage until their rite of passage into manhood at age thirteen. At the end of their schooling, the especially brilliant ones in the class got the opportunity to ask their rabbi for the honor of becoming his follower. If the rabbi said yes, they would leave everything behind and move into the rabbinical compound. For a Jewish boy, becoming a follower was the ultimate honor.

Followers would eagerly sit at their rabbi's feet and absorb his teaching. They would count it an honor to serve the rabbi in even the most menial tasks. They would watch their teacher interacting with people and observe how he handled situations and resolved conflicts. In time they would begin to act, talk, and behave like their rabbi. In fact, if there was more than one rabbi in town, you could usually tell which followers were whose by the fact that they talked and acted just like the rabbi they followed.

"Followers" still exist today in certain segments of Jewish culture. My friend Ed Dobson was visiting Jerusalem on a recent trip, and while he was standing by the Wailing Wall, he saw an aged bent-over rabbi leaning on a cane and walking with five of his young followers behind him.

Each of these younger men was also bent over and limping to the left as they walked — just like their rabbi. Ed knew these men were his followers, because they reflected the likeness of their rabbi — even down to the way he walked!

In biblical times, embracing their identity as a follower meant that the life of a Jewish man would be forever changed. Following a rabbi changed the way they thought and acted, how they responded to life, and how they would make decisions about life. A follower absorbed all he could from his rabbi and lived to reflect his rabbi's teachings and behavior in his own life. There is no doubt about it: choosing the identity of a follower was transformative. If you were a follower, his ways were now your ways, his responses were your responses, his values were your values, and his thoughts were your thoughts.

Understanding and accepting this pattern of following is a tipping point in our quest for effective character-driven leadership. When we accept the identity of a follower of rabbi Jesus, it involves a total submission to his will, his ways, and his wisdom. As followers we count it a privilege to serve him and with deep admiration end up becoming like him. It is in this way that the character of Jesus becomes infused into our lives and leadership. With our being no longer left to lead according to our own fallen ways, our leadership is marked by the compelling ways of Jesus.

But to understand the honor of it all, we need to remember that not everyone had the opportunity to become a follower.

If you were not one of the brilliant ones in your class, you didn't qualify to ask for the privilege of becoming a follower. In a sense you were a loser; you didn't make the cut. So you would leave rabbi school and go back into the trades. In the case of Peter, Andrew, James, and John, they went back to the family business and became fishermen. Being stuck in the dull routines of life as a fisherman, with no hope of ever achieving the honor of becoming a follower, you can imagine what it must have meant for these soon-to-be-disciples to have this emerging rabbi, Jesus, welcome them to a privilege that they never dreamed would be theirs. The invitation to follow Jesus in transforming adventures of thought and behavior was an incredible opportunity for these men. This was clearly an upgrade from casting nets and catching fish. It's no wonder that Matthew says that they "immediately" left their nets to follow him!

The truth is that we, too, are born losers. Born in sin and hopelessly alienated from him, we stand guilty before God, doomed to an eternity without him and hopelessly separated from the presence, peace, and abundant life that are only found in him. None of us make the cut with God. Each one of us is relegated to the trade of living life on our own terms, to the empty pursuit of trying to make our own lives meaningful and fulfilling. Without Christ, we are helplessly and tragically lost.

But then, Jesus shows up in the fishing village of our hearts. Extending his nail-scarred hand, he offers to connect us to the high privilege of becoming a follower of him by forgiving us from the sin that has separated us from God. He welcomes us into an *undeserved* position of honor — a life transforming relationship with him as one of his followers. Loser no more! Who wouldn't abandon our faulted and hollow pursuit of life and leadership on our own terms and gladly embrace the honor of becoming a follower of him?

It is my joy to welcome you to change your sense of identity. To dethrone your instinct to think of yourself as a leader and to accept the transforming *privilege* of seeing yourself as a follower by surrendering your old ways to the ways of Rabbi Jesus. Sit at his feet as he rolls out the Sermon on the Mount. Consider what it means to be poor in spirit, meek, merciful, and a maker of peace. Listen to him call you to be a leader who turns the other cheek, who forgives those who wrong you. To be a leader of a different sort. To lead as Jesus would lead.

Leaders who lead by following take the first step toward character-driven leadership. If you follow Jesus, his unflawed character traits soon become the trademarks of your leadership as well. But the high honor of a life and leadership transforming relationship between a follower and his rabbi rises and falls on whether or not you stay in constant pursuit of Jesus. It is not a one-off commitment. It is a lifelong adventure.

Dynamic #2: Followers actively pursue Christ.

When Matthew uses the word "follower," he literally means to "come after" or "pursue." It's easy to think that being a follower is something passive — as though at some point in our lives we were stamped with the identity of *FOLLOWER* with little or no obligation to actualize what that means as I live and lead.

Understanding that Matthew is envisioning leaders who make Jesus the passionate pursuit of their lives means that all I do in leadership and life is intentionally aimed at closing the gap between my life and the life of the one I follow. It may mean that I need to dump some of my own dreams and pursuits. It certainly means that I deal directly with the sin in my life that keeps me at a distance from him. It means that I surrender to the superior wisdom of his ways and his will. That I pursue the things that he passionately pursues: shalom in the midst of chaos, redemption and liberation of the lost, justice for the oppressed, and the advance uncompromised righteousness in our lives, our leadership, and the cultures that we oversee. The honor of becoming a follower is not just a badge that I wear, but the all-consuming passion of a character-driven leader's life.

Seeing following as a singularly focused pursuit of Jesus is the very essence of authentic Christianity. For many, our Christianity is viewed as a set of boundaries within which we should stay if we are going to be "good" Christians. These boundaries are the rules we are asked to keep, the doctrine that we are asked to believe and protect, and perhaps some traditions of the church we attend. I hasten to say that I am all for the boundaries as long as they are clearly biblical. But if you think that your success as a Christian is measured in terms of staying in the boundaries, you have missed the essence and joy of what it means to be a Christian ..., and more specifically, of what it means to be a follower.

Authentic Christianity, authentic following, is about Jesus at the center of my faith and a hot and tireless pursuit of him. It is about shrinking the distance between him and me on every front. It is about growing to love what he loves and hate what he hates. It is about a relationship that stimulates me to be more holy as he is holy. To be more merciful as he is merciful. And a multitude of other things that followers aspire to in their quest for intimacy with Christ.

True Christianity is first and foremost about a person! Following Jesus means that I live with him at the center of my being and find my highest joy in the adventure of pursuing him.

This would be a great time for you to set the book down and to think through what it is that you are pursuing in your life and leadership. To think through the dreams that conflict with his dreams. To identify the distractions and the obstructions in your life that prohibit your pursuit of him. To recall the price he paid to make you his own, and to know that the real hunger in your soul is for him and not the cheap substitutes.

And, I would like to add, this is not a game of hide and seek! He is there waiting for you. As with the Laodiceans, he is knocking at your heart's door (Rev. 3:20), wanting to come in to dine in a rewarding fellowship with you. Thankfully, his desire for a transformational intimacy means that the joy of pursuing him will be rewarded. And the joy will be experienced in the reality that following him is an adventure in which you will never get bored. He is endlessly interesting and compelling. And endlessly wise and good.

Real-deal Christianity is first and foremost about a person, not about religious projects or principles or even about building great enterprises. Becoming a better Christian, not to mention a better leader, means that I am more in touch with, more like, and more intimately surrendered to Jesus than I was yesterday, last month, last year. Those of us who lose sight of Jesus as the passionate pursuit of our lives and define our Christianity by the boundaries can quickly become unlike Jesus in attitude and action ... particularly toward those who live outside the boundaries. Which would be so unlike Jesus.

Leading as a follower means that nothing competes with Jesus as the defining center of my desires. Grumpy people that we lead, board members who hold us back, challenging situations that seem insurmountable or anything else that we as leaders face ... nothing distracts us from our pursuit of him. In fact, with Jesus at the center, we view all of leadership — its joys and challenges — through the lens of who he is and how we can lead to close the gap between how he led and how we lead.

True follower-leaders see all of leadership as an opportunity to pursue Jesus. In the face of every challenge, every relational conflict, every opportunity to build the enterprise, every temptation and seduction, follower-leaders flee to him, seek his face, and implement his ways. Sharing things in common is an important dynamic in intimacy. The more we have in common with him in our leadership, the closer we become to his heart.

So what would that intimacy look like in the life of a leader?

Dynamic #3: Followers are found in "the Way" with him.

There is one additional nuance to the word Matthew uses for "following." In addition to the concept of coming after Christ, it also means "to be found in the way with him."

Jesus made a bold and unapologetic claim when he said, "I am the way, and the truth, and the life. No one comes to the Father except through me" (John 14:6). We often think of his claim to be "the way" as the way for us to get to heaven. And thankfully, that is true! But saying that Jesus is "the way" means much more than that. It means that he is the way! Jesus is the way to live life. He is the way to handle money. To treat friends. To deal with enemies. To pursue careers. To love family.

And he is the way to lead.

Jesus spent three years of his life, prior to his death on the cross, showing us "the way" to handle a broad variety of situations and encounters. He taught his ways, modeled his ways, discussed his ways, and storied his ways. And he claimed that his ways were the ways of God. It was the claim of divine affirmation of his ways that annoyed the leaders of his day, since his ways stood in direct contradiction to the ways they used to exercise and preserve their power and position.

When Jesus came to our world, he refused to walk in the fallen "ways" of the world. Instead, he took the machete of his divine wisdom and cut new paths through the dense jungle of our confused lives and fallen leadership instincts. These new paths are paths that he himself walked, and he looks over his shoulder and wonders if anyone . . . if any follower-leader . . . is in the way with him.

For instance, Jesus said to his followers,

> "You have heard that it was said, 'You shall love your neighbor and hate your enemy.' But I say to you, Love your enemies and pray for those who persecute you, so that you may be sons of your Father who is in heaven. For he makes his sun rise on the evil and on the good, and sends rain on the just and on the unjust. For if you love those who love you, what reward do you have? Do not even the tax collectors do the same? And if you greet only your brothers, what more are you doing than others? Do not even the Gentiles do the same? You therefore must be perfect, as your heavenly Father is perfect" (Matt. 5:43 – 48).

Notice the contrast between the typical way of responding to conflict and offense and the refreshingly different way of Jesus. We have often heard it said, "I don't get mad, I just get even!" In Jesus' day, word on the street about conflict was the same: "Love your friends, and hate your enemies." It is entirely natural and normal to love your friends and hate your enemies. It requires nothing special or supernatural, no changes or transforming work, to hate your enemies. And in the end, it only adds to the escalation of conflict and chaos.

But peacemaker Jesus has a better way. He invites us to "Love your enemies and pray for those who persecute you." His new way — a way that he himself walked — gets us unstuck from the food fights of life and turns our focus toward blessing our enemies and praying for those who oppose us. An interesting thought for leaders who naturally try to silence, intimidate, marginalize, and retaliate against those who oppose them. And why should we be found in the way of forgiveness, love, and prayer on behalf of our enemies? Because, as Jesus said, the way of God is to love and bless enemies. Is anyone who is reading this book deeply thankful that God loves his enemies? I know I am. That is the meaning of the cross.

And you can hear the sound of his machete cutting a new path of leadership when he tells followers who were grasping for power and prestige that they were acting like the instinctive leaders of their world. He said, "You know that the rulers of the Gentiles lord it over them, and their great ones exercise authority over them." But, he continued, "It shall not be so among you. But whoever would be great among you must be your servant, and whoever would be first among you must be your slave, even as the Son of Man came not to be served but to serve, and to give his life as a ransom for many" (Matt. 20:25 – 28).

Followers follow Jesus in the way of servanthood. They live and lead for the sake of others. They seek to use their position and power to bless others and not themselves. They note the amazing reality that the Creator-King of the universe came to our planet and intentionally chose the identity of a servant and humbled himself to serve all the way to the cross, where he surrendered his rights and privileges as God to serve our deepest needs. And he asks us to cease our journey down the road of self-serving leadership to join him in the enterprise of serving the needs of others!

Whenever we hear Jesus saying, "But I say unto you," or "It shall not be so among you," we hear the sound of his machete whacking a new way through the underbrush of our own fallen perspectives and instincts. He welcomes us to leave the way of greed to join him in the way of generosity (Luke 12:13 – 34). To leave the path of pride and join him on the path of humility (Phil. 2:5 – 11). To exit the way of self-confidence and join him in the way of God-reliance (Rev. 3:15 – 20). Read through the narratives of the Gospels and listen for the sound of his machete! Follow the sound and find yourself in the way with him.

I am fascinated with the fact that the book of Acts notes that the early Christians were known by the culture at large as the "people of the Way." What was the Way? It was Jesus' new style of leading and living. A new way of living that was counter to the cultural values of this world, counter to the sinful tendencies of our hearts, counter to the broad path that leads us far away from God. It was the way of Jesus, and his followers were so committed to his way that even the most casual observer noticed the difference and nicknamed them the "people of the Way"! I wonder if any of those whom we lead would readily identify us as a leader of "the Way"?

Given the privilege for us to exercise the honor of being a follower of him, of living in pursuit of him and of finding ourselves in the way with him, we can't lose sight of the motivation that comes from remembering how very compelling the one out in front of us really is.

HE IS COMPELLINGLY WORTHY

In his account of Christ's call to the future leaders of his kingdom (4:18 – 22), Matthew notes that when Christ approached Peter and Andrew and said, "Follow me," they immediately dropped their nets and followed him. I have always been struck by the immediacy of their response. I'm confident that if Jesus were to interrupt my life and ask me to give up life the way I've been doing it for years, I would at least have to press the pause button and ask a few questions. Will it be hard? Will there be a 401k plan? Can I visit my mother on weekends? Is this a short-term or long-term assignment? And, if I had wanted to sound spiritual, I would at least have asked to have a couple of days to "pray about it."

We have already noted that this invitation would have been considered a great honor for the men being asked. A once-in-a-lifetime opportunity. But there is more going on here than just that.

Why would they immediately decide to follow him? In addition to the honor of it all, it does say something about how compelling a person he is.

Although we are removed from the call of the original disciples by two thousand years, Jesus' call to follow him is just as dramatically interruptive to our lives today. We may have been living in the way that seems right to us, following the advice of others, for many, many years. We have deep grooves of life habits etched in our psyche. If we are leaders, we likely sought out advice and looked for help by reading all the right books. And over time, we have settled into life and leadership styles that feel comfortable. To put it in the context of the first disciples', you've learned how to fish and now you are good at it! So when someone comes along and interrupts that, calling you to learn a new paradigm for life — and for leading — it can feel scary and inconvenient.

Why did the disciples decide to leave everything behind, immediately answering the call? Partly because they saw him as a very compelling person. I believe we must rediscover just how compelling Jesus really is. Scratch the Sunday school image of a meek, mild, humble, and deferring Jesus. Although Jesus is all of those things, the mental image we typically have of him leaves us with the feeling that Jesus is a nice person, but not someone we would want to play golf with. This impression of a Jesus who is merely soft and gentle will never elicit in you the immediacy of a decision to leave everything to follow him.

One thing is clear: The disciples found Jesus to be a compelling person. These were rough fishermen — the "bikers" of their day — and they immediately dropped their nets to follow him. Greedy tax collectors who would have ripped off their grandmother for a bump in their stock portfolio left it all to follow him. A Zealot whose life was dedicated to overthrowing the Roman occupation and restoring Israel to its former glory left the earthly revolution to join the Jesus revolution. To command the respect of men like this, Jesus must have been a riveting person, a man who elicited the attention of others. Real men not only gravitated to him, but ultimately gave their lives for him. Women adored him and felt safe with him.

There was a magnetism about Jesus that drew all kinds of people to follow him. He was authentic, refreshingly different, often challenging the stuffy status quo, and always getting in the face of the self-serving leaders in Jerusalem. And when he taught, something rang true down deep in the souls of those who listened to his words.

In J. R. Tolkien's *The Hobbit*, the dwarves gather to go against the fierce dragon Smaug to get their stolen treasure back. The quest to recapture their treasure promises to be a dangerously frightening experience. But so impressed with his leader, Balin, who is the second in command of all the dwarves, says of Thorin, "There is one I could follow, and one I could call King." Knowing the authentic Jesus should raise the same confident commitment in our own lives and leadership. As the old song says, "Where he leads me I will follow ... I'll go with him all the way!"

Are you compelled by the person of Jesus? Do his words ring true in your soul? Do his actions inspire you to know him, to follow him? Unlike the disciples and the crowds that were attracted to him, you and I now know the full extent of his compelling love for us. We know that Jesus loved us so deeply that he suffered a torturous death for us. We know that he rose again, conquering death, by becoming our champion, doing for us what we could not do for ourselves: canceling the debt of hell, bringing shalom to our chaos, wisdom to our foolishness, and grace to our suffering and trouble. And as if that wasn't enough, he in his abundant mercy has guaranteed a place for us with him in heaven. There is no one who is more compelling, more deserving of our followership than Jesus. And if you choose not to follow him, who will you follow? Has anyone offered you a greater honor than being called to follow our Creator-Servant-King?

So the question remains, will we, like those early disciples who were so taken with him, immediately drop the nets of life on our own terms — and more specifically, the nets of our comfortable styles of leadership — to follow Jesus?

My guess is that most of us who are reading this book have already answered the call to follow Jesus. Yet I know from experience that many who have said yes to his call are still living and leading in the old ways of our fallen perspectives and practices. We are like fishermen who, after being called to something new, have returned to fish again. In a sense, Jesus has taken us to a new lake, but we are using the same old lures, the same old nets! Let's face it: Clinging to our old ways means that we are really not followers at all! Just another leader who is wearing the Jesus fishing cap, but still doing leadership our own way.

I find it interesting that Matthew tells us that "immediately they dropped their nets and followed him" (Matt. 4:20). Why did he reference dropping the nets. He could have simply said, "And immediately they followed him." So what's with the net talk? One thing is clear: As long as they were clinging to their nets, they were going nowhere with Jesus. Which makes me wonder, what are the nets that we continue to cling to that keep us from being fully devoted followers of Jesus? A net is anything that inhibits or prohibits us from fully following him. Only you know the nets that continue to entangle your life and leadership. Perhaps it's the pride that keeps calling you to do it your way, or your unwillingness to forgive a serious offense, or your lack of courage to forage new paths with Jesus, or that secret sin, or your unwillingness to humble yourself to say you are sorry, or the seductive attraction of personal gain and fame that you are unwilling to let go.

I have no clue what your net looks like, but knowing what we know about the incredible honor of pursuing the compelling Jesus by being found in the way with him, why would you think that the nets in your hand were more worthy than he is?

Embracing and actualizing the transforming identity of being a follower-leader is the fundamental character-driven habit of effective leaders.

OUR ALL-WISE LEADER

Devoted followers have learned to instinctively make his ways our ways, his will our will, and his wisdom the "modus operandi" of how we handle the affairs of life and leading.

When his ways seem strange and counterintuitive, remember that Paul reminds us that in Jesus, "all the treasures of wisdom and knowledge" are hidden (Col. 2:3). If "all" the treasures of wisdom and knowledge are encapsulated in him, then who am I to think that I have a better, wiser drill for leadership than he does? Note that he has all the "treasures" of wisdom and knowledge. You can do it your way and operate with the dregs of your own instincts. Or you can raid the treasure chest of the high-value driven leadership perspectives of Jesus.

Which begs the question, "Why are you still reading someone's 'Twelve Steps to Becoming a Great Leader' as though it were the last word?"

So, given the honor of following such a compelling Jesus and given the reality that in him are hidden all the treasures of wisdom and knowledge, why wouldn't you choose to unconditionally follow and gladly embrace him as the singular navigational tool in the outworking of your call to be a leader?

If you find yourself humming the old tune, "I have decided to follow Jesus … no turning back, no turning back!" you stand a fairly decent chance of producing some amazing outcomes. And it will give you the advantage of leading from the platform of moral authority.

CHAPTER 5

BY WHAT AUTHORITY?

Moral or Positional Leadership?

Jesus was the quintessential unlikely leader. He didn't dress like the leaders of his day with their fancy hats and gold-gilded robes. Nor did he hang out with the highly networked to leverage the advance of his cause. He never cleverly maneuvered to get himself ahead, and he was more than willing to risk his political clout by getting into the face of the widely accepted practices of the power brokers. He didn't live in the power-charged neighborhoods of Jerusalem, but settled in the low country where trade routes brought citizens of every nation into the sphere of his influence.

Yet strangely enough, much to the consternation of establishment leaders, people flocked to Christ. He was magnetic. His influence crossed all socio-economic strata and broke through traditional gender and political barriers.

What was the secret?

Jesus' power to influence the masses was generated from the kind of person he was. He was authentic to the core. Transparent, patient, courageous, and above reproach. His life was a consistent example of what he taught. He was clearly the real deal. His teachings resonated with listeners' deepest longings, and his compassion and love made even the outcast feel welcome and safe with him. In the arid landscape of the lower-earth ways of the leadership they were used to, his style was like a drink of cold, clear water. Jesus offered the people a breath of divinely fresh air.

Long after the leaders of his day have passed into brief references in the history books, his leadership remains dynamically alive and well. Now, two thousand years later, his teachings, life, and leadership continue to influence millions around the globe.

Who he was and how he led gave him a unique edge: the edge of leading from the platform of moral authority. And it's that kind of moral authority that gives energy and success to leaders who are actively following Christ.

Leading today with moral authority is no small thing. Never has there been more cynicism about leadership in politics, the corporate world, and even the church. Leaders are often viewed as territorial, greedy, dishonest, self-serving, proud, and a host of other disengaging traits. As was the case in Jesus' day, people are longing for that breath of fresh air in the midst of their disappointment and despair. Finding a leader who offers the cup of cold water they are seeking should happen first and foremost in the church, among leaders who claim to bear the image of Jesus. Only those who, as followers of Jesus, lead with moral authority will be able to tear down the barriers of cynicism and find a welcome mat for influence in the hearts of those they lead.

But leading by moral authority is not the only option. There is an easier, more instinctive option. It is possible to lead simply from the platform of positional authority.

POSITIONAL AUTHORITY

By the very nature of leadership, you as a leader are given the power of position. It's an easy short-cut to choose to lead solely by leveraging the power of your position. If you choose to bypass the character route to leadership, you don't need to worry about effecting leadership through how you lead or who you are as you lead. You have the authority of the position, and as long as that is secure, you can exercise control. Positional leadership is the easy option. Qualities like respect and integrity never have to be cultivated, because you can use the leverage of your position to keep the underlings in line and get the job done.

Leaders who rely on their positional authority tend to be highly pragmatic. Character demands that we live and lead with integrity, but when character is not the driving force, it's hard to resist temptations to cheat around the edges. Lack of transparency, dishonesty, and violation of basic ethics when it serves them well are all a part of the positional leader's arsenal.

Positional leaders value image as a tool to leverage their power. They flaunt the title on their business card, the special parking space, and the nice office and use the power to reward or punish those who serve them. Positional leaders find no value in developing the character needed to command genuine respect and loyalty. Instead, they earn loyalty by promoting and paying their followers well. They motivate them with praise or manipulate them with anger and the threat of withholding approval. They make retaliation a public spectacle so that others learn to stay in line. Lacking a moral compass to guide them, they are free to do whatever is necessary to achieve the desired result. Often organizational insecurity and fear mark the environment of enterprises run by positional authority.

MORAL AUTHORITY

Leading with the platform of moral authority, however, is dramatically different in both its character and outcome. Leaders who possess true moral authority genuinely seek to live and lead with integrity as followers of Jesus. They practice what they preach and try to remain consistent to Kingdom values and principles in the governance of their organization.

People are drawn to leaders with moral authority because of who they are and how they lead. Leaders make mistakes — no leader is perfect — but those who lead with moral authority are humble and honest about their flaws. They repent and admit when they are wrong. They seek successful outcomes, but not at the expense of mistreating people. Instead, they value people and seek to find ways to reward and honor those who serve them. They are humble, thoughtful, patient, and kind. Moral authority leaders create an environment in which followers flourish as people, not just as workers for the organization.

In short, they live and lead in ways that engender respect and admiration.

Leaders who lead from moral authority are trusted, not feared. They are transparent in their dealings, not guilty of covering up. They seek wise counsel from others. They take criticism as an opportunity to evaluate areas in which they can grow. They admit they are wrong. They affirm others generously. They forgive freely. They are reticent to take the credit. They do not foster a culture of "organizational chart" behavior, but rather are willing to see themselves as a servant and to live out their leadership before others as a servant. In short, they attract, motivate, and keep a loyal following based on who they are and how they lead.

You can tell what kind of a leader you are by what people say about you when you are not around. When people praise a leader's character and the manner in which he or she manages, you know there is an element of moral authority at work. But when the men and women in the trenches roll their eyes as the leader walks away, or they try to make excuses to others for their boss's behavior, or they enjoy company jokes about the leader's faults, there is a good chance that the leader lacks moral authority.

Every leader operates somewhere on a spectrum between these two types of authority. But leaders who want to lead like Jesus must constantly resist leading simply from the leverage of their position. They must intentionally cultivate moral authority by fostering a character-driven leadership that engenders trust and respect among those they lead.

POSITION MATTERS

Let me add, at this point, that positional authority is still an important form of authority, yet one that must be exercised with wisdom. Christ himself, while holding no earthly political authority, possessed positional authority as the eternal Son of God As such, he had authority over demonic powers, over sickness and disease, and over the forces of nature. He held a position that was unrivaled. A quick reading of Colossians 1 and Philippians 2 makes this very clear: Even in his humble state as a human being, Jesus retained his full authority as God. But the impressive difference was that he chose to exercise his positional authority, not by spending the power of his position on himself, but rather by using his position for the blessing and benefit of others. Which is why he looked so different from the leaders of his day.

In Philippians 2:5–11, Paul reminds us that even though Jesus held the highest position of authority as God, he was willing to forgo the self-serving powers of that privileged position. Instead, taking on the form of a servant, he humbled himself in obedience all the way to his death on the cross. Jesus shows us that positional authority should not be used to feed our self-serving agendas. Position — whether given to us as a pastor, parent, teacher, CEO, or elected official — is a gift and a responsibility, not something we should exploit for our own satisfaction or affirmation.

Jesus consistently used his position as a platform to serve others and to advance the agenda of his Father. To follow the way of Christ, we as leaders must also empty ourselves of our rights and privileges, count ourselves as servants, and humble ourselves in sacrificial obedience to the ways of Jesus and the agenda of the kingdom. Humbling ourselves to lead as Jesus did may not seem all that rewarding. After all, we all thrive on enjoying the perks of our position, the affirmation, and the applause. But humble obedience and surrender to the kingdom agenda are both the calling and the responsibility of a character-driven leader. Exaltation and reward are God's prerogative to bestow in his time and in his way. It was only after Christ's humble sacrificial obedience that God exalted Jesus and gave him a name that was above every name! This is why Peter writes to early church leaders, "Humble yourselves, therefore, under the mighty hand of God so that at the proper time he may exalt you" (1 Peter 5:6).

But the temptations to discount our character and bypass our submission to leader Jesus for self-advancement and personal success are ever present.

It should not go unnoticed that at the very beginning of Christ's ministry, Satan tried to seduce Jesus to use his position and power to his own advantage. Had he succeeded, Christ would have been like any other earthly leader who leads positionally for their own benefit. These were pivotal temptations — definitive in terms of what kind of a leader Jesus would be.

Satan knew that if he could get Jesus to do his Messiahship according to the ways of Satan, he would strip Jesus of his unique power and derail God's plan to defeat the forces of hell. In other words ... Satan wins!

TIPPING POINT TEMPTATIONS

There are three fundamental temptations that all leaders face. The temptation to use their position and power for their own benefit; the temptation to use their position and power to focus attention on themselves and garner applause and acclaim; and the temptation to compromise integrity to accumulate and acquire spheres of influence that they can manage and control for their own gain, fame, and glory. These are highly attractive options to anyone's ego, and the temptations are particularly seductive to those who have chosen positional leadership as their modus operandi. In a sense, they lack the moral fences to resist the temptation.

Matthew sets up the tension between positional leadership and moral leadership by recording a critical event at the beginning of Jesus' ministry. Jesus has been baptized by John, and with a dove descending on Jesus, the skies have opened with the voice of his Father affirming his pleasure on his son: "This is my beloved Son in whom I am well pleased!" He is then led by the Spirit into the wilderness, where he fasts for forty days. At the end he is weak, hungry, and vulnerable. All of us who have been through wilderness experiences know how vulnerable we are to temptations that divert us from our calling and offer quick fixes to our languishing souls.

Not surprisingly, it is in this season of vulnerability that Satan shows up. The nature of this ambush was clearly aimed at how Jesus would exercise his power and authority.

This is not unlike an earlier ambush in the garden of Eden. Satan is all about moving our focus from a blessed surrender to God to a self-consumed interest in our own prosperity and welfare. The first ambush was in the beauty and blessedness of God's garden. I can't help but notice that this second ambush was in a barren wilderness. A powerful metaphor of the damaging designs of Satan. Satan's outcomes are always intended to damage the landscape of our lives and to defame the glory of our great Creator-God. When Adam and Eve fell to the seduction of living for their own benefit, everything fell around them.

It's a good lesson for us. Leading to use our position and its power for self-benefiting outcomes will inevitably have a negative ripple effect on our own lives, on the environment in which we lead, and on people we manage.

Now, in the second ambush, Satan knows that if he can tempt Jesus — as he did the early caretakers of Eden — to lead for the benefit of himself instead of an unflinching surrender to his Father's plan, he could distract and disable the entire messianic mission.

Here it is in a nutshell. Satan didn't mind that Jesus was the Messiah. He just wanted the Messiah to run the messianic enterprise by the standards and instincts of his dark domain. And, I might add, he really doesn't mind that you are a spiritual leader; he simply wants you to manage the enterprise of your leadership by his ways. He knows that he can distract and disable God's intended mission through you if he can win on this front.

Temptation #1: Use your power to bless yourself.

"Turn the rocks to bread!" was the sinister cry thrown at a tired and hungry soon-to-be leader. "You look terrible and gaunt! Who will follow you when you look so famished? Make yourself a meal, and you can be better at what you are called to do."

But Jesus refused! His mission was to use the power and authority that his Father had given him to bless others, not himself. If he was going to do the bread trick, it would be to feed five thousand men, their wives, and children. His true hunger was to be attentive to every word that proceeds from the mouth of His Father, not to the words of the ruler of lower earth. If he had tasted the bread of his own power, who knows what else Jesus would have done with his power to satisfy his longings and advance his own interests! Would he have called 10,000 angels to rescue him on the cross? Thankfully, he didn't want to set that pattern of ministry behavior as an option for himself.

Jesus wins round one ... but the fight is not over.

Temptation #2: Use your power and position to draw attention to yourself and garner affirmation and acclaim.

Satan takes Jesus to the highest tower of the temple and invites him to do something jaw-droppingly spectacular that will catch the attention of the crowd and prove once and for all that he is the true Messiah. "Jump and let the angels catch you. Then everyone will know you are what you claim to be. After all, didn't the prophets predict that the angels would protect the true Messiah from danger and harm? Prove the point of your greatness! Just imagine the headlines!"

Again Jesus refuses to use his power and position to affirm himself and to garner the praise and applause of the crowd. In fact, Jesus would establish his credentials, not by being "stuntman" for his own glory, but by defining himself in his answer to the disciples of John who asked,

> "John the Baptist has sent us to you, saying, 'Are you the one who is to come, or shall we look for another?'" Jesus replied, laying out the credentials that would authenticate his ministry, "Go and tell John what you have seen and heard; the blind receive their sight, the lame walk, lepers are cleansed, and the deaf hear, the dead are raised up, the poor have good news preached to them" (Luke 7:20 – 22).

As before, Jesus refused to use his positional authority to make a splash for himself as an amazing leader who wows the crowd. Instead, his credentials would be validated by using his position and authority to bless and heal the outcasts, the helpless, and the hopeless.

Temptation #3: Worship me, and I will give you what you deserve!

Not to be deterred, Satan then offers Jesus the best deal of the day. All of the kingdoms of this world, their riches and their glory, could be his if he would simply bow down and worship the tempter. This was no throwaway offer. Someday he would rule the nations! But that would first mean establishing his kingdom through the agony of the cross, paying the high price of disgrace and excruciating pain.

Satan is offering him the spoils of victory without the hard work of accomplishing kingdom outcomes God's way. He can have it all now … the glory, the glitter, the fame and fortune. All Jesus has to do is throw away his allegiance to his Father's path toward glory and exaltation, surrender to Satan, and get it all now. Once again, Jesus establishes his footing and refuses to grab the glory by maintaining his unflinching allegiance to his Father. No shortcuts. No using his power and authority to circumvent the hard work of obedience.

Of all the temptations, this may be the most relevant to us today. It is highly seductive for leaders to accomplish their goals if, when they need to, they can cheat around the edges. Be less than transparent. Compromise integrity. Lie to cover their faults and weaknesses. Take the glory to themselves. Treat people like pawns. Refuse to forgive. And a host of other ways that we can bail on our allegiance to Jesus and bow down to worship Satan to get to our desired ends more quickly and conveniently.

But as relevant as the third temptation is, *all* of these temptations wait just around the corner to radically alter the way we do leadership.

Here was the package delivered to Jesus in a moment of vulnerability: Use the power and authority of your calling to bless yourself (you're hungry, you deserve it); wow the crowd with your abilities (being in the spotlight with much applause will affirm your importance and validate your ministry); and take the shortcut, enjoy the glory and glitter of earthly fame and fortune now, even though you must compromise your allegiance to God's ways to do so (after all, why delay the gratification?).

I can't think of a better analogy for leaders than this wilderness picture. Leadership in many ways is a wilderness. A wilderness in which we are often lonely, misunderstood, unappreciated, second-guessed, underpaid, and the object of gossip and criticism. This creates a self-focus that longs for life in a better way. Gaunt and tired, we too hear the tempter recommending that we use our position and authority to satisfy ourselves. So we succumb and try to navigate leadership to our own advantage, only to find that on the other side of it we are still empty and striving.

Yet, even in the wilderness moments of leadership, the character-driven leader does not fall for the bait.

Like Jesus, the character-driven leader aligns himself with God and the principles of his Word. He does not live by bread alone, but by the ingestion of the Word of God as his navigational tool for life and leadership. He does not put the Lord his God to the test of supporting and blessing foolish and self-centered displays of personal glory. And, for the character-driven leader there is no compromise that is worth the gain of vast ministry empires and the accumulation of fame and fortune.

Character-driven leaders agree with Jesus when Jesus throws the book at Satan by saying, "Be gone, Satan, for it is written 'you shall worship the Lord your God, and him only shall you serve'" (Matt. 4:10).

THE CHOICE IS CLEAR

So the choice is clear. We can lead by the manipulations, twists, and turns of positional authority or by the productive power of moral authority. Maximum leaders choose the latter.

They do so because it is the way that Jesus led and drew people to the enterprise of the kingdom. As followers of Jesus, maximum leaders refuse to lead by pulling the levers of sheer, self-serving power. They value concepts such as servanthood, shepherding, humility, caring and compassion, patience, and a love for the maligned and needy. They value people for who they are, not for what they can do.

Leaders with moral authority understand that they are broken and needy, they mourn their shortcomings and feel sorrow for their sin, they are meek, and they love making things right and doing the right things. Leaders who lead with moral authority seek to make peace among their followers and readily forgive and love their enemies. When given a choice, they will always be true to the Jesus that they follow.

The fact that Jesus had the masses flocking to him is a clear commentary to the power of moral authority. They tolerated the positional leaders in Jerusalem, praised them to their face, and grumbled and made jokes about them behind their backs. You couldn't miss the contrast. The masses loved and willingly followed Jesus. They couldn't wait to hear him teach, and the closer they got to him, the more compelling he became. Only leaders with moral authority compel a loyal following based on the compelling experience of their character and the authenticity of their personhood.

Better yet, leading with moral authority creates an environment where people are drawn, not to the leader, but to Christ. The clearest sign that moral authority is at work is when a leader consistently draws attention away from himself to Jesus

MORAL LEADERS CREATE ORGANIZATIONS THAT CELEBRATE THE PREEMINENCE OF CHRIST

Leaders who lead with moral authority elevate Jesus as the true and singular leader of the organization. None of us can generate moral authority in and of ourselves. We are flawed at the core. So in and of ourselves, we cannot be the ultimate moral leader. Pointing our people to Jesus paints a target that is worthy of all our pursuit. So in essence, the character-driven leader and her people are on a journey to live and lead as Jesus lived and led.

Paul sets the standard in Colossians 1, where he lists the amazing credentials of Jesus and concludes the list by saying, " … that in all things he might have the preeminence." Neither leaders nor organizations get a hall pass on that. If in all things Jesus is preeminent, then he must be preeminent both in my life and in the organization that I lead. His will must dictate the will of our organization. His ways must determine the ways that we do business. His wisdom drives how we apply our knowledge to our environment. And His mission must be our mission.

No matter how strong or compelling a leader may be in his own right, compared to Christ there is no contest. John the Baptist sets the example. Although he made the headlines and drew massive crowds, he said that one was coming whose sandals he was not worthy to untie. He then concluded that, "he must increase but I must decrease."

I recall, as I was walking into church one Sunday morning, hearing a little boy behind me ask his mother, "Is that Jesus?" She said, "No, that's our pastor." I wish she would have said, "No, that's our pastor, but he reminds us a lot of Jesus!"

Leaders who lead with moral authority elevate Jesus as the true leader of the enterprise by turning the spotlight away from themselves to him. And the joy of it all is that celebrating Jesus as the preeminent person in our midst makes leadership an act of worship!

STILL LEARNING

Through the years I have learned some of these lessons the hard way. I hasten to say that I am still learning.

I remember going to the suburbs of Detroit to pastor one of the leading churches in eastern Michigan. I was young and a relatively unknown commodity. The pastoral staff was deep with highly qualified, well-respected individuals who had been at the church for a number of years. The church had an enviable history of great preachers in the pulpit, and I am confident that no one on the staff ever imagined that they would be serving under a neophyte like me. In retrospect, I understand how disappointed they must have been.

In our first staff meeting I said it was important that we begin our work together by giving each other the gift of mutual respect. One of the staff members replied, without looking up as he continued to trim his fingernails, "I think respect is earned, not given!"

The message was clear. I may have been the senior pastor with positional authority, but I had no moral authority. I knew on that day that job one was to live and lead as Jesus did so that at some point they would *want* to follow me rather than *have* to follow me. Establishing moral authority became job one. I have often wished that I could have that day back — that I would have said something like, "You didn't choose me and I didn't choose you, but for reasons best known to God, he has brought us together. I count it an honor to serve with you and look forward to learning from you as we move forward together to advance the work of Jesus." Instead, I asked for something that they couldn't give … yet.

At that same church, the board was composed of long-term members and powerbrokers in the church politic. Since I was young and new to the scene, they often listened politely to my comments, but I could tell that what I said and thought didn't get much traction. Two years into my tenure there, I remember driving home after a board meeting and thinking, "That meeting seemed different. It seemed as if they were listening to and weighing seriously the things I was saying and bringing to the table." I knew that my leadership had turned a corner and that I now had been given the stewardship of moral authority. A stewardship that I could either grow and cultivate or squander by handling it carelessly. I needed to treasure it.

I wish that they had told me in leadership classes in grad school about the importance of moral authority. I wish that they would have clued me in to the fact that when you first arrive as a leader, people will say things like, "We are glad you are here!" and "What is your vision for our future?" But in their hearts their arms are folded as they are asking themselves, "Who are you? Can I trust you? What will you do to us?"

Answering those questions by the way you lead will be the tipping point in the effectiveness of your leadership. If they are answered by the observable growing presence of Jesus in your life and leadership, your future as a maximum leader is bright.

One of the ways we answer these inevitable heart questions is to prove to our followers that we love and value them as individuals, regardless!

Being entrusted with the flock of God is a serious calling. How you treat the sheep as you lead them will be either a deal-breaker or a deal-maker. If you simply see yourself as their leader, you may be in for some disappointing times. If, on the other hand you see yourself as their shepherd, progress is within sight.

CHAPTER 6

WHERE HAVE ALL THE SHEPHERDS GONE?

The Good Shepherd

I love the story of the Sunday school teacher who held up a picture of a squirrel and asked the students if anyone knew what it was. The class fell silent, not sure what to say. As she continued to coax the children for an answer, a boy in the back finally raised his hand. Hesitantly, he said to the teacher, "It looks like a squirrel ... but I think the right answer is Jesus!"

We all know the Sunday school answer is always Jesus. And as we've probed the defining aspect of character-driven leadership, we've found that Jesus is the answer there as well. But it's one thing to say Jesus is the "right answer" to our leadership and another thing to work out the details as we move our character-driven leadership into the messy enterprise of people. When was the last time — if ever — you got past the "right answer" and really drilled down to think carefully about what it means to make Jesus your leadership mentor? More specifically, what would your life and leadership look like if you were to close the gap between your style of leadership and his?

If leading as a follower of Jesus is your goal, I suggest you learn more about what that looks like by sitting with me at the feet of two leaders of the early church — unlikely men who were directly imprinted by the leadership patterns of Christ. Peter and Paul are both great examples of how we can lead and deal with people in ways that reflect the ways of Jesus. In 1 Peter 5, Peter characterizes leadership by using an image familiar to readers of the Old Testament Scriptures as well as congregants in the New Testament church. He describes the role of a leader as that of a shepherd, giving us five traits that distinguish a shepherd-leader who follows Jesus Christ.

Paul, though he does not use the image of shepherding, also helps us more clearly discern the people-related qualities that mark a leader who follows Jesus. Paul summarizes the steps Jesus took to effectively complete his mission in Philippians 2:5 – 11. From the example and teaching of these early church leaders, we have a Jesus-drawn template to duplicate in our own patterns of leading.

SHEPHERD-LEADERS!

Let's begin with Peter's perspective on leadership. As he writes to leaders in the early church, he outlines the fundamental modus operandi that defines how we are to lead:

> So I exhort the elders among you, as a fellow elder and a witness of the sufferings of Christ, as well as a partaker in the glory that is going to be revealed: shepherd the flock of God that is among you, exercising oversight, not under compulsion, but willingly, as God would have you; not for shameful gain, but eagerly; not domineering over those in your charge, but being examples to the flock. And when the chief Shepherd appears, you will receive the unfading crown of glory. Likewise, you who are younger, be subject to the elders. Clothe yourselves, all of you, with humility toward one another, for "God opposes the proud but gives grace to the humble." Humble yourselves, therefore, under the mighty hand of God so that at the proper time he may exalt you, casting all your anxieties on him, because he cares for you (1 Peter 5:1 – 7).

Peter casts leadership in the language of shepherding. As he notes, a shepherd-leader doesn't lead by his own instincts but rather leads like Jesus, under the authority of Jesus, and with accountability to Jesus, the Chief Shepherd.

It's rare to hear a leader articulate his or her role in the language of shepherding. The metaphor of shepherd and sheep is one that most of us are unfamiliar with, and it's a metaphor that seems less leader-like. If you have a push-back response to the concept, it may be because it doesn't communicate the power and authority of models we feel are more fitting to our instinctive sense of leadership. Compared to thinking of ourselves with the image of a corporate executive, thinking of ourselves as shepherds might seem old-fashioned and, quite frankly, a little passive and soft.

So it's no wonder that leaders today look to the corporate model, borrowing metaphors and images from the world of business leadership. Leadership books and seminars tend to describe and define leadership by encouraging even those of us in ministry to see ourselves as executives, basing our decisions on how a CEO would lead. It's interesting to note that many pastors and ministry leaders actually seem to think of themselves, not as shepherds, but as CEOs. Of course, there are aspects of CEOing that need to be exercised. But even in that, the concept of shepherding advises "how" we carry out our executive responsibilities.

I recently heard a leader of some renown recommend that we dump the word *shepherd* from our leadership vocabulary because we are so unaware of what that means in our culture. But instead of dumping the biblical image, it seems better to me to make an effort to recover a proper understanding of the role of the shepherd and how the shepherd image helps us to better understand what it means to lead as Jesus led. After all, Jesus identified himself and his work in the language of shepherding, and he calls us to shepherd as well. So instead of abandoning the shepherding image, let's dig into the Word to discover how we can apply this ancient imagery to our own leadership responsibilities today.

Here are just a few of the identifying marks of a shepherd in the culture of the Ancient Near East:

- Shepherds were among the lowest on the social ladder of their day. They were readily dismissed by those in seats of authority and influence.
- Shepherds were perceived as servants, the "downstairs" folk who took care of the menial tasks of the landowners.
- Shepherds were responsible for protecting and providing for the

prosperity of the wealth portfolio of their masters. Sheep were the measure of a person's wealth, so each sheep was valuable to its owner.

- Truly wealthy landowners had several shepherds, with most of them called *under shepherds*. These under shepherds had to give an account for their sheep and their shepherding to the chief shepherd.
- Shepherds not only tended their sheep, but cared for them, and they often knew their sheep by name.
- Shepherds were responsible not only to serve the master and the chief shepherd, but also to serve the sheep, who by their very nature were weak and vulnerable. Sheep are not at the top of the "brain chain" in the animal world. They need guidance, because they will not look for new pastures on their own, will not return home on their own, and will drown if they try to drink in rushing waters. They are not fast enough to outrun their predators. And their legs are weak and easily sprained or broken.
- Shepherds made sure the sheep were fed, protected, and thriving.

If the idea of using a shepherd to portray a model of leadership seems strange to us today, keep in mind that it was also strange in the time of Jesus. The leaders in Jerusalem craved the applause of the masses and managed their positions for personal gain and glory. "Shepherd" was the last way they would have wanted to be known. Shepherds were anything but well positioned and powerful.

Jesus, being the countercultural, counterintuitive leader that he was, chose to identify himself as the "good shepherd" (John 10:14). And by doing so, he was positioning himself as the servant of the sheep, his people. His responsibility as a leader was to care for his sheep, to serve the sheep with provision, protection, and direction so that they would flourish as a flock. In John 21, Jesus clearly calls Peter — and all Christian leaders after him — to the task of shepherding as well.

We can say many things about shepherds, but one thing is clear: shepherds exist for the benefit of the sheep.

Psalm 23 gives us a beautiful picture of the beneficial care a shepherd offers to his sheep:

The LORD is my shepherd; I shall not want.
He makes me lie down in green pastures.
He leads me beside still waters.
He restores my soul.
He leads me in paths of righteousness
     for his name's sake.
Even though I walk through the valley of the shadow of death,
     I will fear no evil,
for you are with me;
     your rod and your staff,
     they comfort me.
You prepare a table before me
     in the presence of my enemies;
you anoint my head with oil;
     my cup overflows.
Surely goodness and mercy shall follow me
     all the days of my life,
and I shall dwell in the house of the LORD
     forever.

When Peter calls Christian leaders to embrace their call as shepherds serving under the authority of the Great Shepherd, he likely has this psalm in mind. Peter knows that a good shepherd will shepherd his sheep the way the Lord shepherds his people. Shepherd-leaders are focused on their sheep, caring for them, protecting them, and providing for their needs. They do all of this because they know they are stewards of the Master's valuable flock, and one day they will have to give a good account to the Chief Shepherd.

Again, if you see yourself as the CEO of the organization, you will lead as a chief executive. Your focus will be on organizational strategy, on keeping everyone in line, and on mission, budgets, balance sheets, and the enjoyment of the perks and privileges of being the person at the top of the usual organizational chart.

Granted, these leadership functions cannot be ignored. If you are a business leader, you need to be capable in these areas. But if you are *merely* an executive, even a good one at that, your leadership will likely be dominated by the short-term concerns of your business. You might end up losing sight of your larger calling as a kingdom leader, one who leads to develop people. Systems, goals and objectives, programming, vision, and all that a leader needs to manage can easily become the endgame, and people can become cogs in the machine.

Shepherds see their role differently.

At Cornerstone University I need to be committed to exercising my executive authority — not to enable us to build a great university, but to use the university and its resources to build great people. We want to build great students who will graduate and influence the cultures of our world for Christ. We want to create an environment where we can enhance the gifts and talents of our staff and faculty so they can serve the students with strength and joy. The most menial assignment for our campus needs is seen in the larger context of how it enhances the nurture of people. Our mission to produce transformed people who will participate in sharing the transforming power of the gospel globally is all about students ... our sheep. I may have the title "president" on my office door, but I see myself as a shepherd — shepherding the mission of the school and seeking to provide an environment where students, faculty, and staff flourish and thrive.

The Chief Shepherd, whom the writer of Hebrews calls "the great shepherd of the sheep" (13:20), has passionately sacrificed himself to rescue and bless the one commodity that will last forever: people. But people are like sheep without a shepherd. They are often confused, wayward, and wandering. They are thirsty, and they need the water only Jesus can give. They are spiritually poor, blind, lame, and oppressed. Matthew tips us off to the shepherding instincts of Jesus when he writes,

> And Jesus went throughout all the cities and villages, teaching in their synagogues and proclaiming the gospel of the kingdom and healing every disease and every affliction. When he saw the crowds, he had compassion for them, because they were harassed and helpless, like sheep without a shepherd (9:35 – 36).

The books we write, the sermons we preach, the programmatic success we accomplish — none of it will last forever. But the people we serve and lead are all eternal realities. The impact we make on their lives for Christ by shepherding them will last into eternity. Everything else will be left at the border of heaven. People count! And when you think of humankind's needs and vulnerabilities, you know that they — like us — are in desperate need of good shepherding. Leaders are called to be good shepherds on behalf of the Good Shepherd.

DO YOU LOVE ME?

Being Peter was often an awkward experience, but at no time was it more awkward than when Jesus triple-interrogated him in front of his closest friends (John 21).

A little background will help here. After Jesus' death and resurrection, Peter had gone off course and decided to reopen his fishing business. That should be no surprise, because he no doubt was discouraged with the "following Jesus" drill that clearly wasn't turning out the way he thought it would. On top of that, he had just committed an epic fail by denying Christ, and in addition, he was flat broke because Judas had absconded with the treasury. So it's no wonder that Peter was going off mission, off calling ... back to what he knew how to manage and at least yield predictable outcomes. No more unpredictable roller coaster rides with Jesus. Peter knew how to fish, and he knew where the fish were.

But...

After a night of fishless fishing (not a good thing if it's the opening day of your new business), as day is breaking, Jesus shows up on the shore. He carries on a dialogue with the fishless disciples about how the fishing has been. They have no clue that it is Jesus on the shore, but they hear him recommend that they cast their net on the other side of their boat. That must have seemed strange, because they have been fishing all night from both sides of the boat. But when they give the net one more throw, it gets so full of fish that they cannot haul it into the boat. John, astonished, realizes who the man on the beach is and says, "It's the Lord!" And Peter goes overboard and sloshes to the shore to meet Jesus as the other disciples row the boat ashore, dragging the netted fish behind them.

It is here, in front of all of Peter's colleagues, that Jesus asks Peter if he loves him. Not once, not twice, but three times. Each time Peter verbally affirms his love for Jesus. But Jesus is not content to take the words alone without action. If I were to come home some evening and Martie were to meet me at the door and say, "Joe, do you love me?" I would probably answer with a touch of male swagger and say, "Of course, you know I love you!" But if she said, "Joe, I really need to know if you love me!" and then with more depth and intensity asked it again and again, I would know something deep was going on.

Something deep was going on between Jesus and Peter. Jesus had called Peter to follow him, to leave the fish business and focus his attention on people. But now a distracted and discouraged Peter had once again taken life into his own hands and retreated to a more comfortable and predictable way of life. *Back to fishing.*

Before the story unfolds any further, let me note that it is always easier for leaders to lead from what is comfortable, predictable, and more easily controlled. Following Jesus has always been a more challenging leadership journey. But maximum leaders resist the temptation to "go fishing," to lead like old-school leaders. Instead, they lead the Jesus way. The kingdom way. Perhaps reading this book is like Jesus showing up on the beach of your heart, calling you away from the patterns of empty-net leadership to a new and better way.

So Jesus presses Peter to get back on mission, back on calling. Jesus in essence tells Peter that the only way he will know if Peter loves him is if Peter gets back into the people business and leaves the fish and nets behind — again. He says, "Feed my sheep" (John 21:17).

The message is simple. Jesus is saying, If you love me, care about what I care about: the needs and nurture of people ... or as my sons say, "sheeple." Proving our love to Christ by caring about what Jesus cares about should not come as a surprise. That's how we prove our love in our relationships as well.

When Martie and I got married, she suggested we get a dog. I grew up in a non-pet family, thinking that dogs were for people who couldn't make it through life without a prop from the animal kingdom. So that is what I said, which in retrospect was not a good moment in our blossoming relationship. She grew up in a pet family with a black Lab named Trudy. She loved Trudy. And I quickly learned that one way to show my love for Martie is to care about what she cares about. So we bought a dog, and I hate to admit that I even learned to like that dog!

Our love for Christ is proven when we love what he loves ... people and their needs and nurture. It's his love language. It's a scary thought that

I can be all about leadership and busy about the advance of the organization, feeling that Christ must really feel loved by me, when in reality he doesn't feel loved by me at all. My business and spectacular outcomes are not his love language. Christ's love language relates to the people he loves and cares about, and when I make my leadership people-focused as well, he knows how much I love him.

Granted, people-focused leadership — shepherding — can be a challenge. I am all for the person who said that leadership would be a cakewalk if it weren't for people! And I resonate with what a friend of mine says, that the light always draws a few bugs. So proving my love for Jesus by loving what he loves will demand a little grit and determination.

But it's the loving paradigm that enables character-driven leaders to pull it off. Even with the weirdest, least-rewarding people. Shepherds do not care for people because they deserve it or are nice to them in return. Shepherds care for people because they love Jesus. It actually has nothing to do with the sheep and everything to do with my desire to lead as a follower of the Good Shepherd. If he loves them and in fact has paid a great price to make them his own, then they can be precious to me as well — for his sake.

Shepherds care about people … care about meeting their needs … care about nurturing their lives. Shepherds listen well. Mix with the masses. Hang out with the hurting and the helpless. Make themselves available. Are willing to sacrifice themselves to bless others. They make decisions based on what is best for their people. They preach because they love the flock and believe that a word from God is an important way to nurture, care for, and feed God's lambs. They seek to protect, provide, and prosper those whom Jesus loves.

By contrast, outcome-driven leaders find people annoying. They build systems to protect themselves from people and, if necessary, hire others to do the people thing. They surround themselves with a few close colleagues who do their bidding and affirm their actions and attitudes. They love to build relationships with those who can help to get them ahead and network for their success. Everyone else is a nuisance. That may be overstated, but there is a stark difference between a leader who cares about people out of a love for Christ and a leader who doesn't make the needs and nurture of people a pressing priority.

I am concerned for leaders who don't lead to love the flock, regardless of the kind of sheep they lead. It's a head scratcher to me that some leaders surround themselves with entourages and protection as though they are unapproachable. And what does it say about a leader when he or she only goes to the hospital to visit "important" people? Or who only officiates at the funerals of the notable? Or who only performs marriage ceremonies for the kids from high-profile families?

It's interesting to note that in Scripture those who are called to manage God's affairs are almost never referred to as "leaders." They are most often referred to as "shepherds."

Granted sometimes flocks grow to a size where even a shepherd-leader can't serve everyone at the ground level. Staff positions need to be added to make sure that everyone's needs in the congregation or organization are well served. But shepherd-leaders will grieve when they are separated from the very heart of why they serve. Intentionally choosing moments to mix with and be available to people is important for leaders of large organizations. Attend the funeral of someone others think of as a "lowly" member. Officiate at the wedding of someone who has little or even no influence. Look for ways to send messages that you care ... for everyone ... regardless.

CEO leaders build their organization *on* people; shepherd-leaders build their organizations *for* people. You can tell the difference. In shepherd-led organizations, the sheep are thriving, highly valued, and highly motivated followers of the shepherd's leadership. CEO leaders need to crack the whip and often end up leaving people exhausted, highly stressed, grumbling, and complaining. Shepherds have a passion to build people and are accountable to the Chief Shepherd for how they manage their shepherding. CEO leaders see themselves as building a bigger organization and only feel accountable to their own visions and dreams. The masses are insignificant unless they help the dreams come true.

So Peter, perhaps with that early morning fishing encounter with Jesus fresh in his mind, calls us to "shepherd the flock of God that is among you" (1 Peter 5:2). There is an important gut check to the way we lead in this call. The people we lead are not *our* people, nor is the organization that serves these people *our* organization. This is, as Peter says, "the flock of God," God's people organized to advance God's dreams and God's vision. How we as leaders treat his people is a significant stewardship. He paid a great price to make them his own, and they are of high value to him. Ignoring, demeaning, using, manipulating, or abusing God's people is a serious offense to God himself. So at the outset, shepherd-leaders understand that we have been entrusted with the needs and nurture of God's flock and that we serve them as an act of willing stewardship in accountability to the chief shepherd. And when we do this well, Jesus feels loved by us for caring for what he cares for.

Shepherding in God's eyes is no small thing.

Just a couple of weeks ago I had dinner with a graduate of our seminary. As Mark was talking about the demands of managing the multi-thousand headcount church in Indianapolis, he made an important statement. He said, "I never want to get to the place where I lose touch with our people." He then told me that while it was often less than convenient, he intentionally schedules weekly hospital visits and is open to a periodic wedding and funeral of people who are not in the power circle of the church.

Listening to him talk reminded me that Mark had caught the vision of being a shepherd to God's flock. No doubt, Jesus feels loved by him! I have friends who have attended Mark's church for many years. They testify to the admiration and respect that congregants have for Mark as their pastor. Mark is a character-driven shepherd, and it is paying dividends for him and the sheep.

HOW TO SHEPHERD

In the text, Peter lays out a pattern for leading as a shepherd. He gives us five dynamics that should characterize those of us who lead for the good of God's flock.

First, Peter reminds us that shepherds should lead willingly, not out of compulsion (1 Peter 5:2). Shepherding is more than just a job that earns a paycheck. We aren't punching a time clock for God. We are not compelled to lead by the applause of the crowd or the nice people who affirm us. If these are our motives for leading, then what will happen when paychecks, applause, and affirmation disappear?

Shepherds serve with a willing spirit because we love the Chief Shepherd and count it the highest of privileges to be entrusted with his flock. When the phone rings in the middle of the night, we resist the temptation to say, "Take two Psalm 37s and call me in the morning." Instead, like Jesus, we willingly run to rescue lost sheep. A shepherd serves when no one is watching and when there is no personal, immediate reward. Shepherds willingly shepherd the flock because Jesus died for us willingly, and shepherding is our way of saying thanks for the great debt that was paid for us and for the high privilege of being entrusted with his prized possessions.

Secondly, shepherds serve *eagerly* and not for *shameful gain* (1 Peter 5:2). The allure of serving for money and the accumulation of stuff can be seductive traps. I can certainly testify to its fatal attraction. It's easy for CEOs to chase higher salaries and opportunities for larger compensation packages. Most executives see their income level as a validation of their importance. The gain of living in the best neighborhoods, driving luxurious cars, and wearing prestigious watches all play into our sense of worth and self-esteem. Not all of us go into leadership expecting six-figure salaries. Yet the temptation to feel that we should be paid as much as another leader, or that we have somehow been cheated by the compensation committee, can eat away at our souls.

I am intrigued by Peter's comment about gain being a shameful thing. Gain is not sinful in and of itself. After all, the Scriptures clearly teach that a laborer is worthy of his hire. So if the sheep decide to reward their shepherd with gain, that is not something to be ashamed of. It is a blessing from God, who is ultimately in charge of our compensation.

So in what way is gain in leadership *shameful* for a shepherd? I believe the pivotal factor is our motive. Gain is shameful if we are motivated by the gain itself — the money, the power, the trappings of power and privilege — instead of being motivated by the privilege of shepherding God's flock on his behalf. Gain is shameful if it tempts us to do less-than-honorable things to increase our gain. It's shameful if it causes us to feel bitter toward those who are in charge of our compensation. It's shameful if we don't think we need to work as hard or as faithfully because we aren't being paid enough money. It's shameful if we find ourselves trusting in our income instead of the One who provides our income. It's shameful if we spend all our time focused on earthly gain and miss the ultimate eternal reward — the "unfading crown of glory" (1 Peter 5:4) that the Chief Shepherd has in store for the shepherds who serve faithfully. It's shameful if we take another shepherding assignment because it pays more. It's shameful if we cheat on our taxes. It's shameful if we drive our finances into the ditch by going into excessive debt. It's shameful if we see shepherding as a job and our paycheck as our justly deserved reward.

On the other hand, gain in leadership is not shameful if we recognize that God is in charge of our wealth and that in his way and in his time he will care for us financially. As he said to worried disciples,

> "Therefore I tell you, do not worry about your life, what you will eat; or about your body, what you will wear. For life is more than food, and the body more than clothes. Consider the ravens: They do not sow or reap, they have no storeroom or barn; yet God feeds them. And how much more valuable you are than birds! Who of you by worrying can add a single hour to your life? Since you cannot do this very little thing, why do you worry about the rest?
>
> "Consider how the wild flowers grow. They do not labor or spin. Yet I tell you, not even Solomon in all his splendor was dressed like one of these. If that is how God clothes the grass of the field, which is here today, and tomorrow is thrown into the fire, how much more will he clothe you — you of little faith! And do not set your heart on what you will eat or drink; do not worry about it. For the pagan world runs after all such things, and your Father knows that you need them. But seek his kingdom, and these things will be given to you as well" (Luke 12:22 – 31 NIV).

Early in our ministry I helped plant a church of thirty-five people. They stretched their budget to pay us as much as they could, which, as a friend of mine says, often "left a lot of month at the end of the money." By contrast, at this point in my life I don't have to worry about how to pay my bills. I even have a surplus of funds. But I wouldn't trade those early days of scarcity and dependence on the Lord for anything.

We often saw God step in and provide for our needs in amazing ways. Wealthy friends from another town would send us the upscale clothes they had bought for their children once their family had outgrown them. God moved a generous deacon to bless us by taking us out to upscale steakhouses for feasts that we could have never afforded. God taught us to trust in him as our provider and drew us close to him, deepening our sense of his care for us. These experiences stimulated us to worship him more sincerely and provided great lessons for our children. God withheld an abundant supply so that he could show himself as abundantly strong on our behalf.

I recall once, during those days, when I was asked to speak at a church banquet in another state. I admit that I accepted the assignment for all the wrong reasons. It was a shot of adrenaline to my ego just to be invited. I now had an interstate ministry! But I also anticipated a nice honorarium that would help us with our skinny budget. I remember how, after I had finished speaking, I stayed around waiting for an envelope to be slipped to me — an expression of gratitude for the exceptional job I had done. To my dismay, no one handed me an envelope. Finally, as the last person in the room was getting ready to leave, I slipped out to my car and started the long, late-night drive home — grumbling all the way about how expensive the gas had been and the high cost of stopping at McDonald's twice. When Martie asked me how it had gone, I complained that I didn't get an honorarium and murmured about how cheap they were to stiff me.

The next day the Holy Spirit put me in a full nelson and pressed a question on my heart: Why do you serve me? Is it for me, or for gain? Suddenly, I felt deeply ashamed. It was then that Martie and I covenanted that we would never again serve Jesus for money. Nor would we seek to manipulate our service to Christ for personal gain. The next day, after Martie and I had made our life-changing commitment, an envelope arrived in the mail with a generous honorarium. I am quite certain God withheld that benefit just long enough to get our hearts straight!

To this day, we have held to that commitment, and it has been a great joy to see how God has cared for us. On those occasions when I am called to serve without any material reward, I am reminded of our commitment that day and am filled with a fresh eagerness to serve, regardless of the financial outcome. I constantly remind myself that serving Jesus is an act of worship, an expression of my love for him, not a matter of personal gain — and that, in the end, his rewards are "out of this world!"

Peter's third dynamic of shepherding relates to the importance of leading by *example*, rather than by *domineering* over people with an authoritarian spirit (1 Peter 5:3). Peter recognizes that there are two ways to move people forward: You can demand and dominate through threats or manipulative control, or you can live an exemplary life that inspires them to follow you.

Domineering leaders have lots of levers to motivate people to do what they want them to do. These levers give a leader the ability to intimidate, manipulate, play politics in relationships, threaten, and forcefully demand that others do what they tell them to do. After all, they are the ones in charge, and others need to "pick peas or get out of the patch."

Faithful shepherds, on the other hand, motivate people to move the ball forward, not out of power moves, but out of respect. It's that moral authority dynamic. Their lives radiate character and integrity. People watch the exemplary leader and go to school on how they work, how they deal with crisis situations, how they treat people, how they deal with their own failures and shortcomings, how they treat the opposite sex, and how they relate to people who are not like them.

Admittedly, exemplary leadership can be a burden. People are always watching a leader. In one of my favorite leadership magazines, there was a cartoon depicting a carful of people moving down a street when the passengers notice that on one of the house lots there is a house-sized fishbowl with goldfish in it. Someone in the car comments, "That's where our pastor lives!"

Despite the challenges of living in a fishbowl, if we are growing in Christ, being an example is not a burden. It is simply an outgrowth of people watching us mature in Jesus situation by situation, year after year. Exemplary leaders hear people saying that they can see a difference in their leader's life. That their leader is more like Christ than he or she was a year ago!

Clearly, none of us is perfect, but we can be positive examples, leading people by our own desire to grow closer to Jesus. Peter's point is that being exemplary as a leader is not a *liability*, but rather gives leaders *viability*. Leaders don't need to be perfect to pull this off. In fact, when we fail, it gives us the opportunity to model how to handle failure, showing humility and transparency by admitting that we are wrong and seeking forgiveness. When we lead from an exemplary life, respect is the lever that gives us influence.

Paul echoes this point in the leadership workshop he gives to Timothy. In 1 Timothy 4:12, Paul writes, "Let no one despise you for your youth, but set the believers an example in speech, in conduct, in love, in faith, in purity." The word *despise* means to turn our hearts against something or someone. Paul knows that one of the risks of leadership is that the people we are leading can emotionally turn their backs on us, folding their arms against us. In essence, he is talking here about losing respect. It's hard to lead when we aren't respected.

In this case, Timothy's youth was his liability. Our liability may be something else. But Paul advises Timothy to overcome his personal liability by being an example in five key areas. I deal more extensively with this in my book *Shepherding the Church*, but Paul's list deserves at least a brief mention here:

- *Speech:* There are few ways to erode the ability to garner the respect of others more than having an unguarded tongue. On the one hand, speech patterns such as complaining, tearing others down, the use of morally marginal language, gossiping, angry words, bragging, flirting, and the like all work against the moral auhtority of a leader. On the other hand, speaking well of others, encouraging others, affirming your competitors, and speaking lovingly of your enemies all catch the attention of those who listen to you as a leader.

- *Conduct:* The people who serve with you are very much aware of how you conduct yourself. How you behave toward your work, toward those you work with, toward those in authority over you, toward clerks in the stores where you shop, and toward your family, spouse, and enemies. Your conduct will either be an exemplary encouragement to others or an embarrassment to your colleagues. And when you are called out for your poor conduct, how you respond to reproof will also leave a lasting impression of your character or lack thereof.

- *Love:* Do people around you know that you care for them regardless of what they can do for you? Are even "the least of these" convinced of your love for them? Do people see you listening attentively to even the most inconsequential conversation? Do others see you actively looking for ways to forgive and love your enemies? A loving leader will find patience with other people's shortcomings. But a leader who is highly gifted and lacks love will have limited influence.

- *Faith:* Do you have faith in others? Do you encourage them by trusting them with your vision and dreams? Are you willing to let them fail and to help them learn from their failures? People thrive when they know their shepherd believes in them. And do you have faith in God — faith that he will provide, direct, and advise the forward progress of your enterprise? When the chips are down, are you clearly God-reliant and by faith unwilling to let go of him and his promises? Do you have faith that it is he who will ultimately prosper you? And when you suffer, do you have faith that he has a purpose and plan to work through your suffering? Do others see your faith in action?

- *Purity:* It's important to recognize that there is both purity of morals and purity of motives. Your moral purity — or the lack thereof — is obvious in the way you deal with those of the opposite sex and speak about and to them. It is forged by keeping your distance from the subtle allure of sensual enticements. It is forged by loving your God more than you love your own desires. And in case you think you are clever in the way you look at others and that no one will know, you need to think again. Impure actions are more obvious than you think! Having doubts about the moral integrity of a leader erodes people's confidence and trust. And by contrast, observably morally pure habits engender trust and respect. I remember a friend telling me that he trusted a leader so much that he would trust his wallet, wife, and daughters with him, no questions asked.

  There is also the dynamic of purity in your motives. Why do you do what you do? For applause, fame, self-gratification, the thrill of victory, wealth, admiration? And if none of that were forthcoming, would you still do what you do? Or do you do what you do because you feel trapped in the drudgery of being "called" and as such are unable to escape? If you are not in leadership as an act of service and worship to Jesus, then your motives will quickly get sidetracked.

  The church at Ephesus had a long list of celebrated outcomes. But in spite of the admirable outcomes, Jesus said, "I have this against you, that you have abandoned the love you had at first"

(Rev. 2:2 – 4). The problem was that they no longer did the work of the kingdom motivated by love for Jesus as they did at first. It's not unusual to be doing Christ's work for all the wrong reasons, the wrong motives. Purity in motives begins by leading for Jesus' sake as an act of love and worship to his worthy name.

Think of what it would be like to spend a significant amount of time with someone who was exemplary in speech, conduct, love, faith, and purity! There's a pretty good chance you would admire them, want to be more like them, and in fact, delighted to serve with them. It's five steps toward the power and prosperity of moral authority.

There is a choice. We can lead from a domineering position and tell everyone that the beatings will continue until morale improves. Or we can pay attention to the kind of person we are as leaders and compel people to follow us by our exemplary lives. Shepherd-leaders choose to lead by example.

I have made it a practice in my life to seek time and friendship with people who are farther down the road with Jesus than I am. I find them to be stimulating and inspiring. I leave our time together thinking that I want to be more like them. Godly character inspires and motivates people to seek the Lord, to grow in their faith, to pursue the things God loves. In this sense, character-driven leaders are inspirational leaders.

Peter then adds the quality of *submission to authority* to his good-shepherding list of a willing, not-for-gain, and exemplary life. He writes, "Likewise you who are younger, be subject to the elders." It is obviously important for those who are younger to willingly serve under the appointed authorities. Young leaders are often highly idealistic, unrealistic, and sometimes assertive. So there is some protection and an important sanity check for them to be guided by the wisdom of others who have more experience under their belt. More importantly, I am a firm believer that God works through those in authority over us to provide, withhold, guide, and protect us as we exercise our leadership.

Those that blow through the authority that they are under place themselves in a dangerous position. If, when they are thwarted, they scheme to get their way or if they withhold information from authorities in order to avoid oversight, they need to beware. They are on their own! In fact, they have taken themselves out of the arena of God's protection and direction for their lives. Even when our authorities are wrong, a quick look at the story line of Scripture reveals that God uses the mistakes of those in authority over us to do his work in us and through us toward our good and God's glory. Think Joseph! Think of the cross!

And this isn't just for the young leader, although that is who Peter had in mind. Living under appointed authority is a clear directive of Scripture for all of us. Cooperating with authority even when it blocks our dreams and ambitions is the best way to earn the trust of those in authority over us. Bucking the restraints only makes our authorities less confident in our judgment and wisdom. Which only means more trouble down the road.

This does not mean that we can't appeal to authorities or wait for authorities to see things our way. It simply means that we work in cooperation with those in authority over us and not in competition with them.

I can hear someone thinking, *Well, if I would have taken that advice, I would have never accomplished what I have accomplished.* How do you know? Perhaps those in authority would have created a better timing, a better option for you to create even greater things, or a better platform from which you could have succeeded. And even if they hadn't, was it worth eroding your character as you rebelled against them and launched out on your own. You may have gotten a lot done, but you are no longer the person you used to be.

It's the height of arrogance to believe that you are always the sharpest pencil in the box and to think that you don't need anyone to help you guide and direct the enterprise you manage. If Jesus knew that it was necessary to be under the authority of his Father, even to death on a cross, how is it possible that we don't think we need to be accountable to authority as well?

So there it is: leadership from a shepherd's point of view. Through the prism of Peter's shepherd lens, one way to apply character-driven leadership is to love the people you lead as an act of love to Jesus. If they are precious to him, they need to be precious to you, regardless of how "weird" they may be. Leadership is a people-driven venture, and from the Chief Shepherd's point of view, people are the ultimate priority.

People — all of them — need to be loved willingly and not from compulsion; eagerly and not for shameful gain; not with a domineering spirit but by example; and under the authority of those over them. Think of serving a leader you felt was leading because he or she had to, for the money that was in it, and by the manipulations of a domineering hand. Or of watching a leader duck and dodge those in authority over him or her. My guess is that you would be hesitant to follow a leader like that. But if the one leading you was serving with a willing spirit and an eagerness that was not motivated by financial gain, and who inspired you with his or her exemplary life, gladly surrendered to authority, my guess is that you would readily follow that leader. And if that shepherd model is on your mind, you might just be thinking of Jesus, who serves us eagerly, with no thought of earthly gain, and with a surrendered, unstained exemplary character under the authority of his Father that inspires all of us to become more like him.

As compelling as Peter's list of shepherding qualities might seem, there is one that undergirds them all. One without which there is no possibility of measuring up to Peter's concept of character leadership. So he completes his list of shepherding competencies with the fifth character trait, the trait of *humility*.

CHAPTER 7

THE HUMBLE SHEPHERD

What Shepherds Wear

When we think of effective leadership and the necessary traits to pull it off, humility most likely doesn't rank at the top of the list. Effective leadership usually conjures up thoughts of confidence, gravitas, an intimidating presence, and an enviable profile. And while some literature may tip its hat to humility, it is most often viewed as too soft and deferring to be effective. Yet before he is done with his standards for effective shepherding, Peter adds the counterintuitive dynamic of humility. According to Peter, humility is an indispensable quality of effectiveness in terms of both our relationship to God and our relationship with one another. Without apology, he writes, "Clothe yourselves, all of you, with humility toward one another, for 'God opposes the proud but gives grace to the humble'" (1 Peter 5:5).

Humility is what shepherds wear.

Let me dismiss the misgivings that some of us may have about humility. Any thoughts that humble people are quiet, sanctimonious, self-deprecating, passive, always serious, or fading into the background with hands folded in a prayerful posture are all wrong. Authentically humble people

can be the life of the party and still be humble. They can be highly successful and widely acclaimed. Humility is a condition of the inner self at
the deepest levels, and it is planted in the hearts and manifested in the
behavior of a diverse set of people and personalities.

Humility is all about my internal perspectives regarding self and ultimately about my perspective on God's involvement in my success. Nothing
can be more damaging than a leader choosing to take the detour toward
pride.

HUMILITY OR PRIDE

Christ-following leaders must come to grips with the significance of the
damaging potential of pride. The warning is profound: if you are proud,
God will resist you! I always revel in the assurance that "if God be for us,
who can be against us?" (Rom. 8:31). But turning that thought around is
a scary prospect! I find that I have enough headwinds in my own life and
leadership without adding the gale force winds of God's resistance. What
I really need is his wind at my back, blowing with grace under my wings.
The way to guarantee that is to "clothe" ourselves with humility. So let's
see if we can identify where we are on the continuum between a proud
spirit and an authentically humble attitude.

But before we unpack the dynamics of the destructive impact of pride
and the positive influence of humility, let's make sure we are thinking
straight. It is possible that you are reading this as a smashing success from
the world's point of view. You don't sense that you are running into divine
resistance, but rather that you have been blessed by God and that his hand
of approval is on your endeavors. Again, I need to reiterate that outward
success is not necessarily a sign of God's approval. Any gifted leader, secular or Christian, can build a thriving, enviable enterprise. And, as I have
noted — such as with the story of Moses and the water from the rock — in
God's world there are many examples where he has granted success for the
sake of his people and the advance of his kingdom while being displeased
with a leader.

It's possible that God's resistance is not experienced in the larger
picture of the enterprise but in the relationships the leader has with colleagues, others, and other organizations. It's in the trenches where pride

does its ugly work. If a leader leaves a trail of broken relationships, broken people, and hurtful conflict, it's a pretty good bet that pride is in there doing its damage. God's resistance often comes in the form of the repeated reproofs in the form of relational chaos.

So what do proud leaders look like? They believe the best about themselves. They believe that they have the goods to get the job done and that their success is directly attributed to their personal prowess. They bask in the glory of their accomplishments and seek ways to elevate their reputation and recognition. They are impatient with and critical of less-gifted people. They tend to think the way they run their organization is the best way — always. They are highly competitive, seeking to advance themselves at the expense of others and/or similar organizations. Passing out the credit to others is a challenge. They resist critics and take counsel only when it supports their agenda. And proud leaders need to be at the center of the organization, business, or ministry.

It's evident that pride brings with it a whole legion of demons: arrogance, impatience, self-centeredness — to name a few. Pride is at work when leaders use power to advance personal agendas at the expense of others and refuse to accept reproof and correction. Proud people are displeasing not only to God, but to others as well. So it should be no surprise that not only will God resist the proud, but others will resist a proud leader as well.

On the other hand, genuine humility recognizes that all of our gifts and talents are from God, and without the gifting and opportunities that he has given us, we would be nothing, totally incapable of accomplishing anything. Humility readily reflects the glory and the credit away from itself toward God and others. Genuinely humble people are surprised that anything good has come from them. They know themselves, know that they are woefully inadequate in and of themselves, sinners to the core and unreliable without the indwelling Spirit of God to reprove, guide, and instruct them. When they are "good" in what they do and hear the roar of the crowd, they are grateful to feel the joy of God's work in and through them, but they recognize that it is God's work and not their own. Humble people are willing to accept reproof and correction; in fact, they welcome that, knowing how dangerous they would be if left to themselves. They find that praise is awkward and difficult to handle well.

Humble people realize that humility is a choice — a choice to be sane about themselves, who they really are at the core — and grateful for God's amazing grace to equip and use them anyway.

The oft-repeated request, "Pray that God will keep me humble!" is a proud statement. Do you really feel that you are so good that you need an army of prayer warriors to keep you in check? To say nothing of the fact that it is a wrongheaded statement; 1 Peter 5:6 tells us that we need to humble *ourselves*. It is our responsibility to face reality and cease deceiving ourselves about how really cool we are. Pride pushes God to the sideline and makes way for us to step into the spotlight. Instead of God emerging at the curtain call, it's little old me taking the bow. I might give him a nod, but it's "I" who gets the glory. No wonder he resists the proud.

Scripture is replete with stories of God's perspective on the proud. None is more dramatic than Nebuchadnezzar's desire to make an image of himself and to ask all the world to bow to him as a god (see Daniel 3). God sent him into the pasture to eat grass like a beast until he came to his senses about who was really God. Do you like grass? Also, Herod willingly accepted the people's worship as a god. Luke records in Acts 12:23 that when God struck Herod dead, his body was eaten by worms. God resists the proud in many ways, and given God's response to Nebuchadnezzar and Herod, none of us should want to be the object of his resistance.

One of my favorite Mother Goose nursery rhymes is the story of little Jack Horner. It goes something like this:

> Little Jack Horner
> sat in a corner
> eating a Christmas pie.
> He put in his thumb
> and pulled out a plum
> and said, "What a good boy am I!"

So what is Jack doing sitting in the corner? The corner is usually reserved for boys who have not been good. On top of that, he is sitting in the corner with an entire pie on his lap. I have never known a mother to give her son a whole pie! Could it be that Jack has stolen the pie from the kitchen?

And what, may I ask, is Jack doing with his fingers in the food? If you really think about the rhyme, Jack isn't a good boy at all. But he doesn't see himself that way. He thinks he is a good boy. Worse yet, he takes the credit for the plums. Most likely, it was his mother who went out to pick the plums, washed and sliced them, and put them in the pie.

Sometimes I wonder if this is how God sees us when we celebrate ourselves and fail to give him the glory that is due to his name. Every day, you and I live, eat, breathe, and work because of and by means of the grace of God in Jesus. Everything we have is a gift we don't deserve — yet like Jack, we take credit for it all, thinking our goodness has earned it, thinking that we deserve it.

As I am writing this, the Masters Golf Tournament is under way in Augusta, Georgia. I'm trying hard not to leave the manuscript to watch one of my favorite sporting events. This year the Masters will finish on Easter Sunday. As I was thinking about that, I was reminded of the close of the Masters several years ago when Bernhard Langer won the most coveted prize in golf — the green jacket! — also on Easter Sunday. As the interviewer chatted with him while people all over the world were watching, he said to the smiling victor, "This must be the greatest day in your life!" To which Bernhard replied something like, "This is the greatest day in my golfing career, but it is nothing compared to the fact that on this day two thousand years ago my Lord and Savior rose from the grave to give me eternal life." I was almost on the floor with shock and awe. What an amazing moment of humility globally shared from the heart of the most successful person in golf! At the end of the adventure, it wasn't green-jacketed Bernhard, but Jesus Christ who was basking in the spotlight.

I like the way Peter puts this: we are to clothe ourselves in humility one toward another (see 1 Peter 5:5). Just think what a work environment would be like if we weren't competing for the glory ... if we weren't worried about affirmation and praise ... if we were eager to pass the credit around and make worshiping Jesus for all that he has and is doing in and through our efforts our supreme activity. Just think about what it would be like to work for a leader who wasn't always drawing attention to himself, who was encouraging others and not worried about who was encouraging him. And, as Peter adds, we are to wear our humility for all to see. It's like "stylin' for Jesus." In God's kingdom, pride is not in vogue! Humility is the latest fashion trend for up-to-date shepherd-leaders.

When I get dressed, I usually work to make sure that everything matches and that I look good for the day. In my mind I always hit the target. But often, when I kiss Martie good-bye before I head toward the door, she steps back, looks me over, and says, "You can't go out like that! Let me help you." So back to the closet we go for a significant upgrade. When we are wearing the garments of pride, our Chief Shepherd stops us and says, "You can't go out like that." He takes us back to the fashionable wardrobe of humility and dresses us for success in his work. Wear humility well and give him the credit for how you are dressed.

So here is what Peter outlines as the "how" of our leadership. Consider yourself a shepherd. Leave the CEOing to the corporate world. It works well there, but it is disastrous when applied to leading God's flock. Shepherd willingly, not from any external compulsions. Shepherd eagerly, not from any thought of earthly shameful gain. Shepherd from an exemplary life, compelling others to follow you for who you are, not for what you constantly demand. Shepherd from a surrendered heart to the authority God has placed over you, and shepherd from authentic humility, knowing who you really are at the core.

One last key observation from Peter's "character-driven-shepherding" seminar: Note that the leadership model of the Chief Shepherd includes productive suffering. Peter says he was a "witness of the sufferings of Christ, as well as a partaker in the glory that is going to be revealed" (1 Peter 5:1). He then goes on to say that when Jesus appears, there will be a reward for those who have shepherded faithfully according to the pattern Peter has outlined.

The "now and then" dynamic in this text is highly instructive. Jesus suffered to accomplish the mission to which he was called for — namely, "the joy that was set before him" (Heb. 12:2). We are to labor now — and sometimes it will feel like suffering — not for immediate reward, wealth, or fame. Our reward is a far greater reward that will be granted to us when our Chief Shepherd returns: the unfading crown of glory!

While I'm not sure what that will look like or if we will wear it — I don't have a clue what it will actually be — I know it will be far better than any fleeting benefits I may try to accrue for myself in the process of carrying out my service to Jesus. Certainly that crown will be more rewarding than shepherding for lesser compulsions and shameful gain and in a domineering, non-exemplary manner. Coming up empty at the crown ceremony is a poor trade-off for the seductions of self-serving shepherding in the here and now. And speaking of crowns, I'm reminded that the elders in Revelation 4:10 – 11 "fall down before him who is seated on the throne and worship him who lives forever and ever. They cast their crowns before the throne saying, 'Worthy are you, our Lord and God, to receive glory and honor and power, for you created all things, and by your will they existed and were created.'"

Could it be that this is what crowns are for? To give us something of worth to cast before Christ in an act of worship to his worthy name? What a great final act of authentic humility it would be to recognize his ultimate worth by giving my prize to him! And in light of the joy of joining with the elders, it would be a sad day if I were crownless at that event.

As I have often heard my friend Duane Litfin say, "In Scripture it is always the cross before the crown." Shepherding Christ's way in the here and now may be challenging and at times feel like a cross you have to bear, but the rewards for faithful shepherds are out of this world!

While Peter puts character-driven leadership in the shepherding paradigm, Paul outlines the leadership model of Jesus in servant terms. He sees Jesus' leadership style as one that gives up everything that gets in the way of pouring ourselves out to others in humble, obedient service to their needs and to the agenda of our Father.

CHAPTER 8

MINDING YOUR OWN LEADERSHIP

Thought Control

Ilove the female-voiced Siri app on my iPhone! While she no doubt someday will be replaced by a techier system, she does a lot of things for me that I otherwise would have a difficult time pulling off for myself. For instance, if I'm not sure how to get where I need to go, I simply press a button and ask her for directions, to which she normally responds with a map, the time it will take me to get there, and a turn-by-turn voice prompt so that I don't get confused. And if I make a wrong turn, she re-routes me to keep me on track. Frankly, I would have been lost many times without her.

Jesus is the leadership GPS system that enables us to get to the final destination of maximum leadership. Left to yourself, you will be lost!

Once we have chosen to identify ourselves as followers of Jesus, knowing where he is headed is of utmost importance. Thankfully, we are not left scratching our heads, wondering what the ways of Jesus are when it comes to leading.

In Philippians 2:1 – 11, Paul unpacks a compelling model of Christ's leadership. He makes it clear that this is the pattern we should follow in our own life and leadership. He begins by calling us to think the way

Christ thinks, to have the same mind as Christ. He writes, "Do nothing from rivalry or conceit, but in humility count others more significant than yourselves. Let each of you look not only to his own interests, but also to the interests of others. Have this mind among yourselves, which is yours in Christ Jesus" (vv. 3 – 5). Leadership is essentially a mind game. How you think determines how you lead.

Paul tells us *how* Jesus thought about his ministry and how his mind-set dictated his ministry choices. He continues,

> Though he was in the form of God, [he] did not count equality with God a thing to be grasped, but made himself nothing, taking the form of a servant, being born in the likeness of men. And being found in human form, he humbled himself by becoming obedient to the point of death, even death on a cross. Therefore God has highly exalted him and bestowed on him the name that is above every name, so that at the name of Jesus every knee should bow, in heaven and on earth and under the earth, and every tongue confess that Jesus Christ is Lord, to the glory of God the Father (vv. 6 – 11).

COMPETITION IS OUT

The ministry mind-set of Jesus starts with something we should *not* do. We should not lead out of a spirit of competition. This is not an easy temptation to avoid. Most leaders have a nearly irrepressible urge to be on top of the pile, to experience the thrill of the kill. Even as I've led Cornerstone University, I must admit to struggling with this competitive perspective. Within a thirty-mile radius of our school, there are seven other major institutions of higher learning. Comparisons are inevitable, and I have a natural, inner drive for our school to be the most respected of them all. I want Cornerstone to be the best, the destination of choice for the wise and discerning student. This desire is an ever-present tug on my heart.

But the competitive approach to leadership can be like riding a massive roller coaster without a safety harness. Last year Cornerstone won the national championship in basketball. It felt really good to be the best! I was excited to tell everyone I could about it. Shortly thereafter, I had lunch with a distinguished community leader. He told me his son had taken a look at Cornerstone but had selected a different nearby school. That immediately put me in the dumps.

I also serve on the board of another major Christian college that by any measure is the gold standard for Christian higher education. Going to their board meetings, reviewing the financials, and watching them succeed at substantial capital campaigns leads me into a free fall toward covetousness and a touch discouraged when I compare their success to ours.

The leader who leads to compete with others will constantly find himself whiplashed with temptations to change agendas and priorities to try to outdo the success of others.

In secular ventures, a CEO is held accountable for how well he or she competes. It's often a no-holds-barred fight for market share and profitability. But character-driven leaders must resist being driven by competition. As kingdom leaders, they must remember the enterprise of the kingdom is different from the enterprises of lower earth. Kingdom leaders are called to compete against the Evil One and to crash the gates of hell — not each other.

It always bothers me when church-planting strategies ignore the strategic locations of other solid churches and invade territory that is already occupied by allied forces. There is a certain level of arrogance when other churches are written off as irrelevant or unsuccessful, when we think we can do it better or that what our town really needs is "our kind of ministry." Recently I was talking with a church leader who told me that instead of planting in the neighborhood of an existing church, their church was sending leading members and financial support to an existing church in the area they were targeting. They felt called to cooperate and not to compete.

At a recent lunch, a pastor friend of mine was relating a phone call he had from a new pastor in town who was introducing himself. The plant was part of a national church-planting strategy. My friend asked if they had surveyed the town for the need of another church. The answer was no, but that the leaders of the movement had wanted one of their kind of churches in town ... a town that was already heavily churched by gospel-touting evangelical churches. When asked if he knew that nearby there was a good church already in existence, the new guy in town said that he did but that his kind of church was different ... obviously different in a better sort of way.

As soon as the new church was up and running, there was a massive mailing blast to believers in town announcing the new arrival. My pastor friend, who has a highly effective ministry, was not threatened, but was left with a lot of unanswered questions about the seemingly competitive motives of the church-planting strategy that had arrived in his town.

A competitive spirit is what led to mankind's sinful fall in the first place. Lucifer, the angel of light, wanted to be first, to be at the top, aspiring to compete with God himself. For this affront, God cast him out of heaven. He could no longer be trusted there. After his fall, Lucifer entered Eden and told Adam and Eve that they didn't need to be second place either, that they could compete with God, become like him, and win. In that moment, the competitive seeds of sin were planted deep in our hearts, as Adam and Eve gave in to the desire to cease being satisfied with themselves and to become like God.

Opting for a leadership style that is characterized by God's character calls us to lead to cooperate, not to compete. In the Trinity we see three strong and capable persons existing with distinct roles, existing in mutual love and operating as one in unity. Cooperation is the glory of the Godhead! The Father, Son, and Spirit love each other, adore each other, affirm each other, and submit to each other's best interests. They are jealous for each other's glory. It is the prayer of Jesus in John 17 that our lives and our relationships as his people would be "one" just as the Father, Son, and Spirit are one. And this same desire is at the heart of Paul's plea to a divided and highly competitive church in Philippi, to which he wrote,

> If there is any encouragement in Christ, any comfort from love, any participation in the Spirit, any affection and sympathy, complete my joy by being of the same mind, having the same love, being in full accord and of one mind. Do nothing from rivalry or conceit, but in humility count others more significant than yourselves (Phil. 2:1 – 3).

I have found great freedom in the realization that I am not called by God to compete against others. I'm called to accomplish the mission and vision God has given to me and to Cornerstone University. If the kingdom and its forward progress are my greatest desire, then I can rejoice when progress is realized, even if it isn't happening in my little corner of the kingdom. When I return from those "other college" board meetings, I am now free from my own selfish ambitions to rejoice in the great things God is doing there. I am also free to energetically focus on the important mission God has charged me with, to do it for God and not to prove something to myself or to others. As I walk through our campus, I am free to rejoice in the high-caliber students God has sent to us. I am free to be thankful for our faculty and staff. And I am motivated to move the university forward for the sake of God and his kingdom, but not so that we can become better than other schools. I try to save all the competitive energy that resides in my dark little heart for the basketball court, ready to rejoice when our basketball team beats the tar out of our archenemy!

In addition to competition, both selfish ambition and conceit are out as well. There is a natural connection here between a competitive spirit and, as Paul calls it, a conceited heart. Why do we want to compete with others? Could it be that we really want to glorify ourselves above everyone else?

I am convicted by the word picture Paul gives us here. The word for conceit literally means "vain glory." *Vain* comes from the word for "vapor" — and *glory* means that we seek to magnify or celebrate our own virtues. When I put these two words together, I get the sense that we are trying to magnify our nothingness, making much of the fact that we are nothing but a vapor. It's a ridiculous picture. If we start with a little zero and pump it up to be a huge zero, we still have a zero. When we are so self-deceived that we think we are responsible for our own success, we become conceited, self-focused, and sinful.

So how do we fight this instinctive drift toward a conceit-driven competitiveness? Paul tells us to take on the mind of Jesus so that we think about leadership in a Christ-centered sort of way.

"MINDING" OUR OWN LEADERSHIP

Paul goes on in verses 5 – 11 of Philippians 2 to outline the mind of Jesus regarding several counterintuitive ways he lived and led.

Paul describes Christ's pattern of leadership by giving us specific examples of decisions Jesus made as a leader. Paul reminds us that Jesus chose to give up the perks of heaven. He chose to pour himself out so that he could serve us without distraction. He intentionally chose the role of a servant. He chose to humble himself. He chose to become obedient to the point of death, even death on a cross. He chose to wait for his Father to exalt him instead of seeking exaltation on his own. To be a leader in the image of Jesus, to share his mind about character-driven leadership, we, too, have five important choices to make.

Choice #1: Be willing to let go of the perks and privileges of leadership.

One of the attractions of leadership is the lure of the accompanying benefits and privileges. As a friend of mine is fond of saying, "RHIP!" — rank has its privileges. Our world has conditioned us to think we have the right to special privileges as leaders: the size, location, and lush décor of our office. A company car. Generous compensation packages. Extended vacations. Bonuses. The highest recognitions and rewards. We are conditioned to believe that those at the top deserve these perks and special rights. When we seek a leadership position, we are often concerned about the "package." In addition to the salary, what benefits do I get? If I expand the enterprise, how will my contribution be recognized with additional perks?

There is a downside to this, of course. Leaders who think this way tend to be driven by a sense of what they deserve rather than serving out of a love for Christ, responsibly stewarding his work. Immediately inquiring about salary, benefits, and perks as we discuss a leadership position reveals that our primary concerns are material and self-centered. Obviously, at some point it is necessary to discuss compensation. Yet, not only will those who are inviting you to join the cause sense that material and personal benefits are a high priority with you, but they will have the impression that you are motivated by the lesser things of this world. Clearly, there needs to be adequate compensation to support your family, but offers are rarely below that bar. Would you take a cut to go where you felt God was calling you to go? What are the other, more significant criteria you should be exploring long before anyone talks about packages and privileges?

If you are in a situation where you have grown the ministry over many years but in your mind the benefits have not kept pace, then the temptation to figure out ways to line your own pockets as a recognition of your value can create an easy excuse for you to compromise integrity and side-step authority. Hiding income sources, reducing your time commitment to the organization for opportunities on the outside that are financially seductive, restructuring systems of accountability so that only those who are willing to expand your benefits are in charge of the process, sloughing off on the time you invest — these are all temptations to grasp your rights and privileges and to put your material desires above the best interests of the ministry you serve.

The trap of comparison only compounds the problem. There will always be friends and colleagues who are treated better, have more perks, are given trips to Acapulco by people who love them, etc., etc. Nothing can be more discouraging, more disheartening, more distracting than to think that, compared to Mr. or Ms. Gravy Train, "I am underloved and underappreciated."

I recall years ago how tempting it was for me to feel discontent when a friend of mine was asked by his board to chart out how he would like his ministry to be structured in the future. They were magnanimous in suggesting ways they could express their appreciation for his work in the church, and they also asked *me* what I thought they could do to reward *him* for his work and to guarantee that he would continue to serve them. At that time I felt as if my board had been rather nit-picky about my package and rather disinterested in showing me appreciation through their handling of my benefits.

I hasten to say how wrong I was to focus on that and to let it bother me. I have long been committed to the confidence that God is my provider and that he both gives and withholds to accomplish his will in my life. If indeed it is true that ultimately he is the chairman of my compensation committee and that as such works through those in authority over me, I am willing to say with Job, "The Lord gives, and the Lord takes away. Blessed be the name of the Lord" (see Job 1:21). And besides, since when am I in this for money and benefits?

But that long-standing commitment on my part dissolved in the reality of comparison with my friend and his opportunities. He was getting all the perks, and I was not. I finally regained my footing, but it proved once again how deadly it is to focus on perks and privileges. If you want to become bitter toward those who are in authority over you, if you want to be distracted and discouraged by earth-side stuff, then lead others with the thought that you deserve to be well taken care of.

Where would any of us be today if Jesus had diverted his attention from ministry, lured to compare himself to the expansive privileges the high priests and politically connected Jewish leaders enjoyed? Or what would it have been like if he dwelt with a sense of disappointment on all he had given up in terms of heaven's perks to come here? Thankfully, none of that distracted him. Jesus shows us a better way. Being willing to be under the Father's authority — even though foxes had holes and birds had nests, but he, the Son of Man, had nowhere to lay his head — he submitted himself to the high calling of becoming the champion who would ultimately redeem mankind and reverse the fatal damage of the fall. What would you trade for the profound privilege of being a part of that redemptive kingdom mission in the hearts and lives of those you serve? Thoughts of being distracted by the lure of lesser things cheapen the whole effort — to our shame!

Thankfully, Jesus let go of his heavenly perks and privileges to bless and serve us (Philippians 2:6)!

Choice #2: Learn to empty yourself of YOU.

One of the worst things leaders can hear being said about them is that they are "full of themselves." I have yet to meet someone who is special enough to deserve to be full of him- or herself, but nevertheless we are often tempted to think of ourselves more highly than we ought. So to rescue us from the self-deceit of thinking ourselves as overly important, Jesus emptied himself to show us a better way to lead. A "poured out" way to lead.

Two senses are at work here, both of which are highly directive. For Jesus to make himself nothing, he had to give up the voluntary use of his divine attributes so that he could become like us and serve the mission exclusively in the power of the Spirit and under the will and authority of his Father. He poured out the voluntary use of his attributes so that he could be tested in every way just as we are, so that we could be confident that he as our high priest understands our grief, sorrows, and challenges.

If he had used the benefit of, let us say, his unlimited power, his omniscience, and his omnipresence, he could have done a lot of spectacular, self-enhancing things. But he knew that to serve us and show us an example of how we should follow in his steps, he would need to disenfranchise himself from his own power, become dependent on the Spirit, and be surrendered to the will of the Father — just as we need to do as we lead.

If Jesus were to retain his godly advantages, we would have no example of reliance and submission. It would have been all about him; he could have served to glorify himself instead of serving to glorify the Father. In fact, the example that he would have left would be this: Believe in yourself, your capacities and competencies, and do the will of the Father to your own glory and credit.

Making ourselves nothing means that we, too, serve the mission of the Father without the intrusion of the drive of our personal dreams and passions. It means that we have emptied ourselves of all pride and self-centered ambition and that we are fully reliant on the Spirit to empower our gifts and talents, fully surrendered to the Father's dreams, plans, and purposes. Those of us who refuse to empty ourselves will end up competing with the Father and believing that what we have accomplished has been a credit to how clever we are rather than to the Spirit's work in our lives and leadership.

I am struck with Paul's words to the Corinthians. Though highly capable in and of himself, he writes,

> For I decided to know nothing among you except Jesus and him crucified. And I was with you in weakness and in fear and much trembling, and my speech and my message were not in plausible words of wisdom but in demonstration of the Spirit and power, that your faith may not rest in the wisdom of men but in the power of God (1 Cor. 2:2 – 5).

Of all the spiritual disciplines, emptying ourselves should be the most regularly exercised. We need to get good at emptying ourselves of self-indulgence, self-promotion, self-pity, self-affirmation, self-centeredness, and all the rest of the self-obsessed dynamics that make leadership all about us and not the Spirit's power through us to the glory of God.

Once we have emptied ourselves of ourselves, we are ready to trigger the second sense of this "pouring out" choice Jesus made. There is no doubt that in three years of ministry, his legacy was built on the fact that he constantly was pouring himself out on behalf of others. With the resources of love, mercy, grace, kindness, and advocacy for the poor and marginalized at his disposal, he refused to be stingy and poured out these benefits in abundance to those he ministered to. His pouring out of himself provides the example for us to follow, as we too can be found with him pouring out the resources of his grace that so many around us need. Empty of self, I am both ready and capable of being filled with the Spirit (instead of myself) and of turning my attention to the needs of those around me. To, as Paul says, "In humility count others more significant than [ourselves]" (Phil. 2:3), which prepares the way for us to effectively follow Jesus in implementing the next choice into our leadership style.

Choice #3: Lead by being a servant.

As we let go of our perks and privileges and empty ourselves of ourselves so that we can pour into the lives of others, we are free to engage our leadership as servants.

As I have said, I have studied a lot of theology and have been taken with fascinating biblical truths. Yet, over time I find that I have grown accustomed to their grandeur. But I will never grow accustomed to the amazing mystery that when God came to my planet in the person of Jesus, he intentionally chose the identity of a servant.

Jesus could have set up a throne in a specially built palace and worn glorious robes bedecked with jewels and trimmed with the finest gold. His crown could have been lavish enough to create envy in the heart of every world leader, and he could have surrounded himself with masses of blazingly strong angels to serve his every need. He could have demanded that all humanity make the trek to Jerusalem and bring expensive gifts and pay homage at his feet. And it would have been right; he deserves that. He is God! Instead, he chose the identity of a servant. Strange as it sounds, he would be our Servant-*King*.

Can any of us get our heads around that? Hardly. But as we have noted, if Jesus had come to serve himself as intuitive leaders do, none of us would have been rescued from our sin. Because he chose to be a servant, our journey to hell has been canceled, and heaven is now guaranteed.

Servants focus on the *needs of others*. They train themselves to anticipate and see needs and then give their time and talents to meet those needs. Their lives are outwardly focused. They find fulfillment in blessing others. They encourage their followers, send notes of congratulations and affirmation, spread the glory around, and publicly affirm seemingly inconsequential efforts. Servants find their greatest joy in seeing others succeed.

Servants also serve those in authority over them, willingly and eagerly. They carry out, with energy and enthusiasm, the wishes of those to whom they are accountable. Servant-leaders serve the mission of their organization by protecting it and advancing it. They seek the best for the entire endeavor and are willing to sacrifice their own advantage for the greater good.

In short, this affirms that the mind of Jesus about leadership always drives us outside of ourselves into the arenas of human need.

Let me underscore again that this does not mean that we as servant-leaders undervalue our organizational position or power. Jesus intentionally chose to live and lead as a servant, yet he never gave up his *position* as God. But he chose to use his position and the power of his position to serve and to bless even the lowly and marginalized. Servanthood is most powerfully expressed by those who hold a high position. We expect individuals down the organizational chart to serve — what choice do they have? But when a leader exercises her position in a way that sacrifices her own interests for the welfare of others, she sends a clear message to others about the nature of her leadership and her commitment to lead as Christ led.

I have never seen an organizational chart that reflects the reality of servant-leadership. Most charts are shaped like a pyramid with the head person at the top. Everyone serves the position above them and, ultimately, everyone serves the man or woman in the nice office at the apex of the chart. But if we let Jesus advise our organizational chart, the pyramid would be upside down. Leaders see themselves at the bottom of the inverted pyramid, serving one layer of people, who serve the next larger layer, who ultimately serve those who in effect make the organizational dreams come true. In this organizational chart, the real heroes are those at the top of the inverted pyramid. They are the people who end up fulfilling the mission.

I recently had the chance to visit the manufacturing plant of Request Foods, Inc., and walked through the plant with Jack DeWitt, founder and CEO. Jack leads a thriving company that produces and distributes millions of food products a year. As we walked through the plant, Jack greeted people on the line by name, stopped to talk with them, asked how their ailing parents were doing, and patted them on the back. Clearly, Jack knows his employees and he cares about them. You can count on this: that business thrives because of the serving spirit Jack expresses to others. He uses his position to transfer value and worth to those who work for him. It's no wonder that he is a success.

One day while I was serving as president of the Moody Bible Institute, I was riding the elevator to the ninth floor, where my office was, watching a short housekeeper trying unsuccessfully to reach high on the inside of the doors to clean the fingerprints off them. It would have been easy for me to think, "Pity that some ordinary employee didn't get on this elevator. They could have helped her. But this is not what presidents do!" Or I could ask to take the squeegee bottle and rag and finish the job for her as we ascended to my destination. Knowing that I needed to use my position to serve, I proceeded to help her get the job done as others got on the elevator at other floors. I remember seeing her a few weeks later and asking her how it was going. She beamingly said, "Great! Everyone is helping me with the elevator doors!"

When leaders serve, it's contagious. Others take notice, and it changes the way they think about their role.

Dietrich Bonhoeffer often referred to Jesus in his writings as a "man for others." It was obvious to all who walked with Jesus, and to all of us who observe him today, that he meant what he said to a group of followers who were clamoring for big-shot spots in the kingdom: "The Son of Man came not to be served but to serve, and to give his life as a ransom for many" (Matt. 20:28).

I wonder, would it be obvious to those you work with and to those who are in authority over you that you, too, have come to serve and to give your life for others?

Choice #4: Lead through humble obedience.

As I mentioned at the beginning of this book, I am often asked what my biggest challenge is as a leader. In my position at Cornerstone University, there could be many answers to that question: the need for a growing enrollment, guaranteeing the school's financial stability, fund-raising, guarding the mission and vision, keeping the culture positive and thriving … and the list goes on.

But, as I have already said, I am aware that in actuality my biggest challenge as a leader is me. Keeping my ego in check, making sure that my walk with the Lord is not stagnant and ineffective. Staying attentive to the need to follow Jesus and to honor his will and his ways in the way that I carry out my leadership. Keeping my thoughts pure and managing my weaknesses and fallen instincts. These are all alligators in the swamp of my life that I need to continue to wrestle into submission. I am very much aware that if I'm not careful, I could be the biggest problem at Cornerstone. I need to humbly discipline my life in obedience to God so that I can effectively serve.

So it doesn't escape me that to carry out his leadership successfully, Jesus humbled himself and became obedient to his Father — an obedience that led to his own death. We have discussed at length the ramifications and importance of self-imposed humility. But let me add that the essence of humility is the willingness to surrender to authority even if it means the death of our own dreams and agendas. And again, it's not that we can't appeal to and plead with authorities to see things our way. Jesus pled with his Father in the garden of Gethsemane to permit him to avoid the agony of the cross. But when he realized there was no other way, he obeyed at a heavy cost to himself.

At the heart of the choice to humble ourselves is the essential ingredient of surrender. Surrender to our Father in heaven to carry out our leadership according to his will and his ways. Surrender to the mission he has prescribed for us and our organization. Surrender to the needs and nurture of others. And it also involves a willingness to die to ourselves and our self-consuming drives and desires. Surrender is humbly saying with Jesus, "Not as I will, but as you will" (Matt. 26:39) in every aspect of our leadership.

Recently I viewed a DVD of a church service in Mexico. As the preacher passionately called the church to repentance, a man stood up and started waving a white hankie. Then another stood, and another, until seemingly the whole congregation was waving white flags of surrender with tears running down their cheeks as they turned their wills over to the Savior. Character-driven leaders keep a white hankie in their pockets, and when tough life or leadership situations tempt them to renege on their resolve to lead with the mind of Jesus, they take them out and humbly wave them in surrender to their Servant-King!

Choice #5: Be willing to wait for exaltation.

In our text in Philippians 2, it is clear that humble obedience, even to the point of suffering, always precedes exaltation. There are no shortcuts. As we have seen, we are called to live and lead in faithful obedience to the ways of Jesus, and our exaltation will come from him in his time and in his way.

The amazing thing about Jesus is his clear determination to serve the will of his Father regardless of the approval and applause of the crowd. As Paul says, Jesus was willing to deny his own need for personal affirmation and to serve all the way to a cross as a rejected criminal. But in due time the Father poured out affirmation by giving him "the name that is above every name, so that at the name of Jesus every knee should bow, in heaven and on earth and under the earth, and every tongue confess that Jesus Christ is Lord, to the glory of God the Father" (Phil. 2:9 – 11).

Character-driven leaders who lead with the mind of Jesus resist the temptation to lead for their own exaltation. Let's face it: the desire for exaltation is no small thing! It is what we all want — to be recognized and valued for who we are and what we have done. But the pattern in our text is clear. Our first priority is not the reward of recognition and exaltation, but the humble willingness to surrender — with joy — to the will and ways of Christ our leader, even when surrendering seems counterintuitive, difficult, and unrewarding.

There is no doubt that words of affirmation are the love language of most leaders. But I have learned that if I serve for affirmation and the affirmation doesn't come, I feel deflated and lose the edge for serving Christ with energy and ambition. I guess that proves that the biggest struggle underneath it all is that serving for the reward of exaltation makes my leadership all about serving for "me" and not for Christ.

Take preaching, for instance. It is most likely one of the key places where we preachers feel a pressing need for some sincere "attaboys." I have found that whether or not anyone else affirms a sermon, the most important voice of affirmation is Martie's. If on the way home she says, "Joe, that was a great sermon! God really used it in my heart," then what others say or don't say becomes irrelevant. It is her affirmation that counts. For us as leaders, leading for Jesus is like that. It's his affirmation that counts. And when we faithfully lead not for ourselves but for him, then be assured that affirmation will come to us in his time and in his way.

When we circle back to Peter's paradigm for shepherd-leadership, he ends the instructions for how we are to lead by calling us to "Humble yourselves … under the mighty hand of God so that at the proper time he may exalt you" (1 Peter 5:6). Exaltation is God's business; humble obedience is our responsibility.

I have no idea how or when God might exalt you. It may be through an unsolicited affirmation that comes from someone who has been blessed by your leadership. It may be from those in authority over you as they are impressed and grateful for your servant attitude and diligent service to the organization. It may be when he hands us one of those unfading crowns of glory. Or it may be in eternity when you hear, "Well done, good and faithful servant!" But what I do know is that he asks that I not lead to exalt myself, but to exalt him and his glory through my leadership, and that in due time he will exalt me.

The choice we face is clear: We must decide whether we will lead for self-exaltation, seeking honor now, or as Jesus did, pursue the emptying of ourselves as we serve in humility, anticipating the day when God will exalt us. Which will it be?

It is obvious that the biggest challenge to kingdom leadership is the issue of who is the driving force at the center of my life and leadership. If I am at the center, then I will lead from lesser, damaging compulsions. I will seek to dominate others for the sake of accomplishing my own agenda and resist the thought that good leaders are humble leaders. I will lead to compete to win. Thoughts of giving up my perks and privileges will be unwelcome thoughts. Making myself nothing by pouring out myself to others will go against the grain of all that is shouting within me to not surrender to God's will and ways.

But if Jesus is at the center, then it becomes about him and his way to live and lead. Following the path of leadership that he as the Chief Shepherd and Servant-King has prescribed is the highest pursuit of character-driven leaders.

PART 3

A REDEFINED LEADER

Core Competencies

CHAPTER 9

WHICH KINGDOM?

A Sermon Worth Listening To

At first glance it's hard to see Jesus as a maximum leader. He was an outsider, either ignored or rejected by those who made things happen. Those in his closest inner circle were less than highly distinguished, and in the end he was crucified as a criminal in naked disgrace. Not your usual profile for a highly successful leader. But then ... three days later, his story flipped, when through the agony of the cross and the disgrace of seemingly epic failure he rose to conquer the enemies of sin, death, and hell — and became our champion. Without the cross and empty tomb there would never have been ultimate victory.

In this light we should never judge a leader whose journey seems unlikely, who may in the moment look like a failure, whose work may not seem to be measuring up to the speed and sophistication of other leaders. He or she may, like Jesus, be following the counterintuitive kingdom essentials of character-driven leadership. And nowhere are these kingdom competencies for leadership more clear than in Christ's Sermon on the Mount.

Before we delve into those kingdom competencies, here are a few thoughts about the sermon, its context, and its nature.

TWO KINGDOMS

From God's perspective, there are only two kingdoms: the kingdom of this world and the kingdom of heaven.

The kingdom of this world is ruled by Satan, who is, as Jesus described him, "a murderer from the beginning, and does not stand in the truth, because there is no truth in him. When he lies, he speaks out of his own character, for he is a liar and the father of lies" (John 8:44). This means that Satan's kingdom is managed by misinformation, lies, distorted values, and death. Not a reliable system from which to lead.

By contrast, Paul says that God's kingdom "is not a matter of eating and drinking but of righteousness and peace and joy in the Holy Spirit. Whoever thus serves Christ is acceptable to God and approved by men" (Rom. 14:17 – 18). The kingdom managed by Jesus offers to bring peace to our chaos, rightness to our wrongness, joy to our sorrow, healing to our brokenness, truth to the confused, and hope to the despairing. These are God's dynamics from which the kingdom is managed and led.

As a leader you must decide, ultimately, which kingdom you will serve — the kingdom of this world or the kingdom of heaven. Which kingdom's values will be represented in your leadership? It will be either one or the other. There is no middle ground.

THE KINGDOM'S CONSTITUTION

The Sermon on the Mount is Christ's delineation of the ways and wisdom of the kingdom of heaven. It is the constitution, the ethical code, of the realm over which Jesus is King. It expresses the values that are fundamental to kingdom living and as such serves as an outline of the will of the King in both our lives and our leadership.

Christ's words give us hints of what life will be like when his kingdom is in its full, eternal glory. But the sermon he gives isn't just something for the future, a yet-to-be-experienced reality. Through his life, death, and resurrection, Jesus has inaugurated the kingdom in us, and in his life and teaching he demonstrated how to live by its principles. When he healed the sick, gave sight to the blind, and raised the dead, these amazing feats of power were more than just evidence that he claimed to be God.

These miracles were a living picture of what the kingdom of heaven looks like on earth. Through them, Jesus proved that his kingdom would break the back of sin and its consequences and restore health and wholeness to people damaged by the fall in a fallen world. His ministry proved that through him the kingdom brings healing and hope to sinful men and women, destroying the grip of the fall and restoring lost and broken souls to their intended wellness. It is the brilliant light of Christ's shalom piercing the darkness of Satan's domain.

Jesus' demonstrations of the kingdom's power and presence were a sneak preview of eternity. As we follow the ways of Jesus, kingdom leaders are also called to make the kingdom of Jesus visible in our fallen world, giving those around us a glimpse of the kingdom that *has* come and *will* come in fullness when Jesus returns. While we may not have the power to make the blind see and the dead come alive, the more significant end results of peace with God, shalom in the midst of chaos, the healing power of love and forgiveness, and the blessed effects of mercy and grace to lost and wayward souls are all kingdom realities that are well within our grasp. The Sermon on the Mount charts for us the ways in which we can answer Jesus' prayer that his kingdom would come on earth, as it is in heaven.

I grew up being taught a theological system that relegated the Sermon on the Mount to a future time. In retrospect, I feel cheated by that system. It taught me to skip over these principles, only applying them eschatologically as part of God's end-time plans. Because of this, I tended to ignore their impact on my life personally and felt no impulse to bring them to bear on my sin-bound world.

Thankfully, someone pointed out to me Paul's statement in Colossians 1, which says that Christ has already placed me in his kingdom — *now*. As Paul notes, "He has delivered us from the domain of darkness and transferred us to the kingdom of his beloved Son" (Col. 1:13). I began to understand that there is an "already, not yet" reality to the kingdom. So while the Sermon on the Mount gives us a glimpse of what the kingdom will be like when Christ's rule is established over all, it is also a guide for kingdom living in real time in the here and now.

This was good news for me — and challenging news as well. I joyfully embraced the truth that I had been placed in the "kingdom of his beloved Son," but I also realized that I no longer had excuses for ignoring the counterintuitive, countercultural patterns of life and behavior Jesus taught his followers as citizens of the kingdom.

In its broadest sense, the gospel is the good news that the King has come and has inaugurated a kingdom that will ultimately conquer evil and erase its consequences, restore lost souls to his fellowship, and place us in the new Eden, where righteousness, peace, and joy will prevail.

What does this have to do with character-driven leadership? Everything! If we wish to be maximum leaders — leaders who welcome the lost to enter the kingdom, lead them under the authority of the King, and participate in the kingdom agenda of bringing shalom and healing to the chaos of this broken world — then we need to live and lead as kingdom leaders by the principles and practices of the kingdom. As a friend of mine says, our lives and leadership should be a sneak preview of the really big show to come!

The only other option, because there are only two kingdoms, is to lead in the way of Satan's kingdom. For me, it's not a choice; it's a given!

KINGDOMS IN CONTRAST

What would our leadership look like if we led by kingdom values?

It wouldn't be a bad idea if we thought of ourselves as the appointed governor over an outpost of the kingdom, one that exists in enemy territory. Our mission would be to manage our territory so that it resonates with the will of the King and shines with the glory of the kingdom, as a light in a dark and decadent land. In his book *The Jesus Way*, Eugene Peterson describes how this perspective — living as representatives of the King — can make a radical difference in our life and leadership. Peterson writes,

> We live in a world where Christ is King. If Christ is King, everything, quite literally, everything and everyone, has to be re-imagined, re-con-figured, re-oriented to a way of life that consists in an obedient following of Jesus.[3]

We fail miserably in our outpost mission if we manage kingdom territory by the will and ways of the "Philistines" around us. But that is what

---

3. Eugene H. Peterson, *The Jesus Way: A Conversation on the Ways That Jesus Is the Way* (Grand Rapids: Eerdmans, 2007), 9.

we, as Christian leaders, are often tempted to do. Again, Peterson diagnoses the problem:

> North American Christians are conspicuous for going along with whatever the culture decides is charismatic, successful, influential — whatever gets things done, whatever can gather a crowd of followers — hardly noticing that these ways and means are at odds with the clearly marked way that Jesus walked and called us to follow.[4]

He goes on to say, "Doesn't anyone notice that the ways and means taken up, often enthusiastically, are blasphemously at odds with the way Jesus leads his followers?"

Peterson concludes by pointing out that "success" — attracting large numbers of people or seeing visible results — does not necessarily validate our methods. In response to those who may insist that their success validates the ways and means whereby it has been attained, he writes,

> The one positive thing that can be said for the ways and means approved and rewarded in this world is that they work, sometimes magnificently, in achieving grandly conceived ends. Wars are won, wealth is accumulated, elections are won, victories posted. But the means by which those ends are achieved leave a lot to be desired. In the process a lot of people are killed, a lot of people impoverished, a lot of marriages destroyed, a lot of children abandoned, a lot of congregations defrauded.[5]

Jesus raised up an army of followers so that they would live and lead in a *new* way — the kingdom way. That way of leading and ruling stood in sharp contrast to the way kingdoms in his day were ruled. For example, Herod's kingdom was managed and reinforced by intimidation, manipulation, and military might. His glittering palaces, built on the backs of Hebrew slaves, stood as a symbol to his fame, wealth, and power. Everyone bowed to Herod and praised him in public, but privately they despised him. To maintain his power in light of the arrival of a potentially rival king, Herod had every male child under the age of two slaughtered. He was brutal and ruthless. He led with the frightening power of his position.

Israel itself was ruled by the chief priests, who had politicized their positions by buying and selling them in the courts of Rome. They used their

---

4. Ibid, 8.
5. Ibid, 9.

priestly positions to accumulate great personal wealth. They flaunted their status with fine linens, robes decorated with gold, and headpieces that caught the attention of the crowd. As stunningly impressive as all of this was, the average Jew on the street saw the chief priests as distant and out of touch with the everyday realities of life. This is why the writer to the Hebrews assures us that *our* high priest isn't like the well-insulated, out-of-touch, high-rolling religious leaders of Israel: "We do not have a high priest who is unable to sympathize with our weaknesses," he writes, "but one who in every respect has been tempted as we are, yet without sin" (Heb. 4:14 – 16).

Then there were the rulers of Rome, a worldly empire governed by carnal and unrivaled power. The emperor was considered a god, and his armies forcibly maintained the peace of Rome with their intimidating presence. The world in which Jesus lived belonged to the powerful and highly positioned. Everyone else bowed in quiet subservience — or they paid the price.

By contrast, the emerging kingdom established by Christ operates on a far different frequency. The last are now the first. The poor are blessed. Servants rule. The humble are honored and exalted, while the proud are resisted. The wealthy struggle. Power is to be ascribed to the meek, and mercy and justice trump the personal manipulation of power. In Christ's kingdom sinners have worth and value and are the object of loving pursuit, while the self-righteous are warned and scolded for their religious pride. To live you have to die, and to gain you have to give away all you possess. All Jesus taught about life in his kingdom is directly opposed to our normal, natural ways of thinking in the kingdom of this the world.

In fact, when Jesus proclaimed the ways and rules of the kingdom, people were confused. Some were put off. As Robert Farrar Capon writes in *Kingdom, Grace, Judgment,*

> Mention Messiah to them and they would picture a king on horseback and not a carpenter on a cross; mention forgiveness and they would start setting up rules about when it ran out. From Jesus' point of view, the sooner their misguided minds had the props knocked from under them, the better. After all their yammer about how God should or shouldn't run his own operation, getting them just to stand there with their eyes popped and their mouths shut would be a giant step forward.[6]

---

6. Robert Farrar Capon, *Kingdom, Grace, Judgment* (Grand Rapids: Eerdmans, 2002), 7.

Remarkably, not much has changed in two thousand years. The way of Jesus is just as countercultural today as it was then. If we are to be authentic kingdom leaders, we need to carefully evaluate the way in which we lead as well. If we lead by the instincts that come naturally to us, or by the accepted norms of the world, then we are probably leading in ways that align with the purposes of that other kingdom, the kingdom managed and manipulated by the Enemy of God, Beelzebub himself.

Thankfully, God has not left us to wonder what the Kingdom way is like. Telling us what it is not like, he reminds us, "My thoughts are not your thoughts, neither are your ways my ways" (Isa. 55:8), and he tells us, "There is a way that seems right to a man, but its end is the way to death" (Prov. 14:12). Then patiently and clearly he lays out for us the dynamics by which life and leadership in his kingdom are expressed and experienced.

John Stott, commenting on the Sermon on the Mount, notes that it

> is probably the best-known part of the teaching of Jesus ... and certainly it is the least obeyed. It is the nearest thing to a manifesto that he ever uttered, for it is his own description of what he wanted his followers to be and to do.[7]

There is good reason why this sermon is the best-known teaching of Jesus — and the least obeyed. Its principles and directives challenge our normal, natural ways of thinking. And applying the principles of the sermon to leadership is far from easy. Jesus tells us to do things that in our natural selves seem weird and counterproductive. He says that we should love our enemies and pray for those who persecute us. He tells us that generosity, not greed, is the way to true wealth. That we gain, not by accumulation, but by giving away what we have.

Obviously, it takes thought and reflection, as well as some trial and error, to learn to faithfully apply the teachings of Jesus to our context as leaders today. In the next chapters, we will look at six of the eight Beatitudes. The meaning of these verses is an important beginning for would-be kingdom leaders. They deal with core kingdom attitudes that prepare us to trigger the life-specific prescriptions in the remainder of the Sermon.

---

7. John R. W. Stott, *Christian Counter-Culture: The Message of the Sermon on the Mount* (Downers Grove, IL: InterVarsity Press, 1978), 15.

CHAPTER 10

RELIANT AND REPENTANT

Dealing with Self-Sufficiency

C hrist's articulation of the kingdom way for life begins with eight qualities of life that are non-negotiable marks of blessed kingdom people. If they are celebrated kingdom qualities for kingdom living, then how much more important is it that they be the hallmarks of kingdom leadership.

If we understand followership, we are well aware that you can't separate how you live from how you lead. Live wrongly, and you will lead wrongly. Live well, and you will lead well. If Jesus is our navigational instrument for life, then the same Jesus and the same principles are our navigational instrument for leadership. So, as much as they advise how we live, they must also advise how we lead.

The eight essential life-leadership competencies are called the Beatitudes. People who practice them discover that their lives are blessed by these qualities and rewarded with significant outcomes. This list of competencies is a measuring tool for leaders who want to lead as Jesus did and who seek to lead with the moral authority with which he led.

So let's get started.... In a no-holds-barred blast to our normal thoughts and patterns, Jesus begins with an amazing statement. I guess he figured he would weed out the proud and self-reliant ones at the outset — because, from Jesus' point of view, kingdom leaders would be ... *poor in spirit.*

RELIANT

"Blessed are the poor in spirit, for theirs is the kingdom of heaven" (Matt. 5:3).

Think of opening a bestselling leadership book that begins with the importance of leaders being "poor in spirit." Quite simply, that would not happen. In fact, quite the opposite: We would read that effective leaders need to be strong in spirit, confident, bold, and self-assured. They need to dress, act, and speak with gravitas. They need to carry and project the weight of their office with dignity and to be fearless visionaries who can pull off dramatic turnarounds and upwardly spiraling growth trajectories. They are heavyweight problem solvers. Words like *capable, wise, savvy,* and *instinctive* are the kind of words we would want to put into the profile for the ideal candidate for the headhunter to find.

By contrast, Jesus is looking to bless those who are just the opposite ... who are poor in spirit.

The words that Jesus uses are highly instructive. The word recorded in Matthew actually means "poor," as in those who beg. Not just those who don't have much money. Being poor in this sense means that we are destitute and in desperate need of help. This flies in the face of the delusion that leaders are to be confident and capable in and of themselves. It calls for leaders to recognize that they are in desperate need of others to supply them with the wisdom and resources to live and lead effectively. Most specifically, that they need God to guide and direct them with kingdom wisdom and power.

To take this seriously we need to have a realistic view of ourselves. All of us are fallen, broken, failing, and prone to wrong-headedness. Given that I was born in sin and that this sinful state has radically disoriented me from what is true and right, I often remind myself not to trust my instincts. As I have already admitted, my first instincts are most likely wrong — thus, left to myself, I would tend to make a mess of most things. When I am offended, my first instincts are not to forgive and not to seek ways to express love to my enemy. I do not instinctively love the unlovely; I do not instinctively resist self-serving impulses, nor do I suffer graciously. My proneness to self-protection, self-fulfillment, and personal pleasure tends to distort every event and every relationship. When I honestly access my true condition, I begin to realize that I am impoverished at the core and in great need.

It's not that we don't have gifts and talents that inherently enable us to lead. But when we are honest with ourselves, we recognize that even those have been a gift to us from God. That's why we call them "gifts" and why we speak of "giftedness." Without God's bestowing them, we would be nothing and totally incapable of doing anything of worth and value.

More discouraging yet, since we have been given the gifts, our fallenness tends to distort how we use them: most often for our own good and gain, and not for his glory. So even the most gifted of us are debtors, owing an unrepayable debt to God. Who gave us the gifts, the temperament, the doors of opportunity, the brain, the calling? In reality there is no such thing as the self-made leader.

PROUD OR POOR IN SPIRIT?

From this vantage point, being impoverished in spirit is not a hindrance but a great asset. It saves us from the jeopardy of ourselves. It makes us dependant on God for clear instruction about life, relationships, money, and organizational principles. It makes us willing to seek counsel and guidance. Because we know how frail we really are, it becomes possible for us to admit that we have been wrong and to seek restoration and future guidance. It enables us to approach our tasks and our leadership humbly. It instills gratitude toward God for his assistance and to those who help us succeed. In essence, we become a leader who is transparent, honest, open, and realistic.

As such, we also set an example for all others who are fallen comrades. People gravitate toward leaders who refuse to wear the mask of "I'm okay, and as your leader I know what is best." Being poor in spirit gives leaders moral authority, because they are not taken with themselves, but are willing to open themselves to their need for God and the support and sustenance of those around them. It makes leaders surprised when they succeed. And it makes it easy to pass the bouquet of praise to others who have made a donation to the poorest of the poor ... the leader himself.

On the other hand, leaders who do not acknowledge the poverty of their spirit fall prey to all the characteristics that rob them of moral authority and force them to the old school leadership ways of empowering themselves with their position, their gifts, their cleverness, and their manipulative strategies. Since they see themselves as great leaders because of their own competency, they see all of their success as a result of their own prowess. They are not prone to easily give credit to others, let alone to giving God the glory.

These leaders often see themselves as the smartest among those with whom they work ... and perhaps the smartest in their field. They believe in their instincts and are resistant toward those who challenge their ideas and practices. They believe that since the success is directly attributable to their leadership, they should be affirmed and rewarded. When the affirmation is not sufficient enough, they feel cheated and devise ways to make sure that people see and celebrate the greatness of their work.

They are proud in spirit.

I have always been struck with the story of Jacob. It is the story of cleverness, competence, and the unusual capability of Jacob to manage his environment to his advantage. Until, that is, the situation arose where he had no capacity to do that. Meeting his brother, whom he had cheated, would probably mean that he would be a victim of his brother's punitive wrath.

Scripture tells us that the night before he met Esau, Jacob wrestled with God ... physically. He pleaded with God not to leave him until God blessed him. Perhaps for the first time he realized that he was poor in spirit, incapable in and of himself to face the impending crisis. And God did bless him. Not by giving him the power to defend himself against Esau, but rather by making him lame and God reliant. He now had no choice but to fully trust God for his success and deliverance. He was now poor in spirit and God reliant. God rewarded him by melting Esau's heart.

For leaders who think of themselves as competent in and of themselves, the best thing that God could do would be to touch the thigh of their self-confidence and make them fully reliant on him for guidance and success. You would know that you have come to your senses about life and leadership if you stop singing, "I did it my way," and were overheard humming, "I need Thee, oh, I need Thee; Every hour I need Thee! Oh, bless me now, my Savior, I come to Thee!"[8]

Character-driven kingdom leaders should make this old church song the anthem of their leadership: "Spirit of the living God, fall afresh on me. Melt me, mold me, fill me, use me. Spirit of the living God, fall afresh on me."[9]

You will know that a leader is poor in spirit when she thankfully admits that God's favor has advanced her success and she is delighted to give the glory to God.

And the outcome? *"For theirs is the kingdom of heaven."* Leading by our own capabilities and instincts will inevitably lead us to create our own kingdom shaped after our own dreams and desires. But being fully reliant on Jesus and leading by his ways will enable us to reap the benefits of enterprises that reflect the kingdom of heaven. Poor-in-spirit leaders have no other option than to lead the kingdom way and build ministries that reflect the kingdom. To the best of their ability in Christ, they live and work in a kingdom environment and experience the kingdom blessings of righteousness, peace, and joy.

Interestingly, being poor in spirit sets a leader up to succeed in Jesus' second core essential for kingdom leadership.

REPENTANT

"Blessed are those who mourn, for they shall be comforted" (Matt. 5:4).

If you initially winced at being "poor in spirit" as a leader, the thought of being mournful as a kingdom leadership quality may be equally unsettling. According to lower-earth instincts, leaders should be happy, upbeat, joyfully leading the charge!

But once we understand what Jesus is inviting us to, we realize what a necessary ingredient this is for kingdom effectiveness. And, it needs to be

---

8. The chorus to the hymn "I Need Thee Every Hour" by Mrs. Annie S. Hawks (1872).
9. "Spirit of the Living God" by Daniel Iverson (1935).

noted, leaders who "mourn" don't necessarily go around in sackcloth and ashes. In fact, they can be mournful and still be a positive, upbeat leader leading the charge with joy.

"Mourning" is the natural and, in fact, healing response to tragic events in our lives. It is the emotion prompted by significant loss. Mourning is the emotion that drives the spirit to do everything in its power to ensure that an event of tragic proportions does not happen again if it can be helped. Mourning the loss of a loved one drives us to love more deeply the ones we love who are left behind. Mourning is the emotion that accompanies failure and that drives us to live differently so that we will never fail again.

Interestingly enough, the word *mourn* in this context is a reference to our mourning over the failure of sin ... corporately, nationally, and more specifically, over our own sinfulness. It means that kingdom people are blessed when they experience mourning deep inside because of the tragic nature of their sinfulness and its consequences, its deep offense to God, and its negative impact on the lives of those around them.

Mourning is the alarm bell of the presence of sin in our lives that drives us to do something about it and to guard ourselves against doing it again. In Psalm 32, David relates going through a deep season of mourning over his sin of adultery and murder. It caused him to flee to God for forgiveness, where he discovered the comfort of God's restoring and steadfast love.

When leaders mourn over their sinfulness, they recognize the seriousness of sin and identify with God's own reaction to sin. It again makes them aware of their frailty. Mourning our sin keeps us humble, and as Paul states in 2 Corinthians 7:10 – 11, it drives us to repentance. It is a guard against further sin and as such leads us to holiness.

MOURNLESS LEADERS

Leaders who take sin lightly rarely mourn. Having rationalized their sin and having used it so regularly for their own advantage, they no longer hear the alarm. They are hardened to its presence and numb to its consequence. A mournless heart frees them to compromise what is right for self-advancement, both personally and organizationally. Mournless leaders resist reproof and accountability. They only mourn when they are caught. And when they are caught and reproved, they seek to transfer blame. If trapped with evidence, they only admit what has been discovered, hoping to get off with the least punishment possible.

After stifling the urges to mourn, over time their hearts become hardened and the built-in engine of a godly response to sin increasingly loses steam until there is no twinge of mourning left to lead them to correction and restoration.

Leaders who are unwilling to mourn their sin are often caught in the web of the delusion that as a leader they will lose respect if they admit they are wrong. Actually, everyone knows that leaders are human and frail. Not recognizing sin and dealing with it is how we lose respect.

On the other hand, those who mourn over their sin align themselves with God and seek comfort and restoration in him. As David did with Nathan, they respond positively to the reproofs of life that God brings into their lives. In fact, true mourners will want to deal with their sin even *before* they are caught. They welcome accountability so that they will sin no more and detest the failure that drew their hearts away from what is right.

Mourning leaders are willing to do what is necessary to be reconciled to God and the community. Going to those they have wronged in their sin and seeking forgiveness without transferring blame or excusing the failure is the mark of a true mourner. They do not hide the details that have not been discovered. They are ready and willing to admit that they have been wrong. And their mourning spirit reminds them of how frail and fallen they are so that they feel a deep need to rely on God and others (poor in spirit) and are propelled to the blessed state of hungering and thirsting for righteousness.

In short, mournful leaders "get it." They feel and respond to the weight of sin, repent, seek restoration, and flee from it. In so doing, their lives serve as a mentoring influence on others who need to know how to deal with sin as well.

On a Sunday morning early in my ministry, I walked into my office and opened my briefcase to pull out my sermon notes. As I started going over my outline to prepare to mount the pulpit to proclaim "the truth" of God, I was deeply convicted by the thought that I had just lied to one of the church leaders to get myself out of trouble. As the Sunday school superintendent, he had asked me if I had ordered the next quarter's

Sunday school material. He had reminded me the week before, but I had completely forgotten. So, without thinking twice, I said "yes" to protect myself from looking irresponsible. After all, I was the leader, and leaders are responsible people.

The unrest in my soul was a genuine mourning of my sin. The alarm bell was unmistakable. I mourned over what the event said about myself, that I could lie to him so easily. I mourned over the fact that I was a spiritual leader who had just compromised my ministry to preserve my fallen sense of self-respect. I mourned that I was getting ready to serve God through preaching and that I had grieved God through my actions.

I couldn't shake the turmoil. The mourning drove me to resolve it — to ask God to forgive me. That was the easy part. The next step was tough, yet necessary. I went out into the foyer and asked the man and his wife to come into my office, where I acknowledged my sin and asked for their forgiveness. Graciously, they forgave me. I found comfort in their response and a deep resolve to sharpen my commitment to truthfulness even when it means that I will lose face. I had experienced the comfort of forgiveness and the fact that "godly sorrow brings repentance" (2 Cor. 7:10 – 11 NIV).

The ability to embrace and value the quality of a mourning spirit that leads to repentance, restoration, and righteousness finds great inspiration in a full awareness of God's desire to forgive and restore.

OUR FORGIVING FATHER

My mind races to the story of the prodigal son in Luke 15. In this story Jesus makes it clear that the real sin issue was not the naughty things the young man did in a far country, but rather the direct offense that his choices were against his father. It was the deepest of offenses in that culture for a son to ask for his inheritance ahead of time. It was like saying to his father, "I wish you were dead." Taking the portions of his inheritance and cashing out the assets was also an offense in that the value of the estate was a part of the father's income for the later years of his life ... his "Social Security."

On top of that, the young man wasted all the money on riotous living — parties and prostitutes — in a gentile land. The point Jesus was making is that when we sin, whether we get caught or not, it is a deep offense to our Father in heaven.

How will an offended father respond? The mourning in his spirit for the consequences of his sin brought the prodigal to the end of himself and drove him to return to his father and beg forgiveness and restoration. As you know, the father meets him and, unlike the prevalent prodigal stories that would tell the listener that the father would severely beat the wayward child and make him pay for the offense, this father weepingly receives the son back again, throws a party, and kills the fatted calf.

Trusting God's steadfast love for us regardless of our sin and believing that he is waiting to receive, wash, and restore us should propel us to reject the delusion that since we have been clever enough to get away with and cover our sins, everything is okay. It's not. Even if our sin is undiscovered, we have already deeply offended the most important person in our life. Yet, his love for us should wake us up to the fact that our Father knows and that, separated from him in our sin, we are wallowing in the pigsty of failure in ongoing offense to the One who deeply cares. Getting up to flee to the Father's lavish forgiving love is our only healthy option.

Character-driven leaders who lead with moral authority reject the hypocrisy of taking sin lightly and of being a law unto themselves. They value mourning, hate sin in their life in any form, and live to grow in righteousness. They stay in a mode of repentance.

When Martie and I were first married, we bought used pieces of furniture. It was my job to refinish them so that they would be presentable additions to Martie's decorating scheme. When I had a hardwood table to refinish, it was a very rewarding experience. I would take the tough stripper that would eat all the old finish away and reveal the raw wood. Then I would sand it with rough sandpaper. Then I would strip it again to remove any residual layer or old varnish. Then I would sand it with a slightly lighter sandpaper. Then when it was flawlessly smooth, I would put a coat of polyurethane on it. When it dried, I would sand it again. Then I would put another coat of polyurethane and sand it again. I would do that repeatedly until it was restored to its original beauty and usefulness.

I think that, in a sense, this is what God does with repentant leaders. Our evident sins are stripped away, and as he reveals ongoing, sometimes hidden sins, he continues to sand and polish our lives, making us more and more useful and beautiful reflections of his character and glory. Living repentantly as an ongoing openness to his continuing refinement is a major advantage to the advancing effectiveness of our leadership.

Living repentantly keeps us reprovable, honest, humble, and consistent. It enables us to lead from a platform that says, "In reality we all are co-strugglers against our fallenness; follow me as we go arm in arm toward victory."

And the outcome? *"They shall be comforted."* Mournful leaders are comforted by the forgiving grace of God and the pleasure of a clean conscience.

Reliant and repentant … two lead character traits of kingdom leaders!

CHAPTER 11

MEEK AND RIGHTEOUS

Being Right in All the Right Ways

If it weren't for people, we could all be very successful leaders. But people tend to get in our way. Especially those who are not like us, who don't like us, who don't agree with our decisions, who oppose our dreams, and who criticize and complain about us! Unfortunately, these kinds of people are a lot like the poor: they will always be with us. So the solution is not wishing they would go away, but figuring out how to successfully lead with them in the pack. Jesus' recommendation? Be meek and righteous.

MEEKNESS

"Blessed are the meek, for they shall inherit the earth" (Matt. 5:5).

Like *reliant* and *repentant,* the counterintuitive nature of this leadership quality is striking. Like poor in spirit and mournful, meekness does not make the top ten traits of a successful leader in lower-earth wisdom literature. To most of us, meek people are too deferring and fearful to get anything productive done. No one really wants to follow a supposedly cowering leader whom others can steam roll over and take advantage of.

So why would Jesus put meekness as #3 on his list of non-negotiable, countercultural, counterintuitive kingdom competencies?

To be meek, in terms of the meaning of this word in Christ's day, means to be gentle, kind, humble, considerate, courteous, and appropriately deferring and forgiving to those who oppose and offend you. And for all of us who would think that meekness may actually do more harm than good in moving an organization forward, you need to remember that Moses himself was regarded as meek above all others; that Jesus described himself as being meek and lowly in heart; and that Paul described Jesus as meek and gentle (see Numbers 12:3; Matthew 11:29; 2 Corinthians 10:1). Two stunningly effective leaders in my book who were characterized as being meek.

After all the leaders who reject meekness and get their way by lording it over others, leveraging their power in strong arm tactics, angry threatening outbursts, holding grudges, and demanding restitution are long forgotten, the names of Moses and Jesus will still rank up at the top of the list of the greatest leaders of all time.

So, what would it mean to be authentically meek as a leader, and in what ways would it help you establish a base of moral authority?

First, it would mean that in the way you speak and act, you have a gentle spirit. Your leadership would not be characterized by being bombastic, crass, cruel, or insensitive. You would not be known for speaking poorly of those who don't agree with you and of verbally cutting down those who are not like you and or not in sync with the way you do business or ministry.

Meek leaders listen carefully and thoughtfully process the ideas and input of others. They seek to see life and work from others' points of view. They are not impetuous or uncaring. They take seriously the feelings of co-workers and honor ethnic differences. They have long ago stepped off the pedestal of their own self-importance and have elevated Jesus as the worthy center of all that they are and do. As such, they defer constantly and gladly to him. As we have mentioned before, they agree with the highly acclaimed evangelist John the Baptist who said, "He must increase, but I must decrease." They defer to the worth and value of others as he has commanded. They are attentive to the needs of the poor and weak ... even those who can do nothing to help the leader's initiatives.

Meek leaders willingly live under the authority of Christ. Boards of thoughtful, talented individuals are welcomed to speak into the meek leader's life and practice. They readily seek the advice and counsel of others and are willing to sacrifice themselves to seek the good and welfare of all.

They never make themselves look good by making others look bad. They are not quick to judge. They are not arrogant. They willingly live out the mind of Christ by following Paul's admonition to do "nothing from rivalry or conceit, but in humility of mind count others more significant than yourselves. Let each of you look not only on his own interests, but also to the interests of others" (Phil. 2:3 – 4).

They abhor the prevailing tendency of leaders to promote themselves and their notoriety.

They don't mind being seen as a shepherd — or as a servant, for that matter.

They have a great capacity to bloom where they are planted and to trust that the Lord will exalt them in due time (see 1 Peter 5:6).

Meekness, in short, is the appropriate attitude of humble deference to the people, systems, and structures that exist in the environment of the leader. It works itself out in kind, gentle, courteous, and considerate attitudes and actions that fill the community with the kingdom hallmarks of righteousness, peace, and joy. The now-familiar words of Paul remind us that

> the kingdom of God is not a matter of eating and drinking but of righteousness and peace and joy in the Holy Spirit. Whoever thus serves Christ is acceptable to God and approved by men. So then let us pursue what makes for peace and for mutual upbuilding (Rom. 14:17 – 19).

Meek leaders humbly seek to infuse righteousness, peace, and joy into their culture and as such are acceptable to God and approved by men.

But one of the most distinguishing marks of meekness is a willingness to deal peacefully and productively with those who oppose, criticize, and offend the leader. Instinctively we seek to silence, discredit, and marginalize those who speak against us. We find ways to retaliate against those who oppose and offend us. When others speak against us, we speak poorly of them to even the playing field.

Meekness knows nothing of these kinds of responses. In fact, meek leaders have learned the productive skill of turning their enemies over to

God and seeking ways of loving them in return. Totally counterintuitive, but totally what it means to lead as a follower of Jesus.

THE MEEKNESS OF JESUS

In one of the most exemplary cases of the meekness of Jesus, Peter describes Christ's response to his taunting and reviling enemies on his way to the cross. Peter tells us that "He committed no sin, neither was deceit found in his mouth. When he was reviled, he did not revile in return; when he suffered, he did not threaten, but continued entrusting himself to him who judges justly" (1 Peter 2:22 – 23). Peter prefaces that amazing reflection of meekness from the life of Jesus by saying that "Christ also suffered for you, leaving you an example, so that you might follow in his steps" (v. 21).

I can't imagine Jesus yelling back at the riotous masses shouting to crucify him, or threatening Pilate with the wrath of God if the Roman governor doesn't defend him. As silly as that seems, it often is the kind of response that leaders who face hostile situations express. And while we normally don't yell, we do seek ways to get back at those who oppose and offend us. We can marginalize them, speak against them, rally our friends against them, fret and plot about ways that we can deal with them ... the list of tactical revenge tools is long.

Perhaps it has never crossed our minds that God may have sent those who oppose us into our lives for a reason. Before responding to detractors, meek leaders stop to ask if God is speaking to them through the offense and to patiently seek to discern what God is doing through the conflict. Meekness responds positively to reproof. Those who harden their hearts to reproof resist the loving and productive hand of God in their lives.

What a wonderful freedom there is in a meek leader's life when he is able to hand his enemies over to God. Think of the joy of being free of the entanglements that inevitably come from fighting back. More wonderful yet, think of the power of the good that comes when a leader returns good for evil and blesses those who curse him.

It is what Paul was after in Romans 12:16 – 21 when he wrote,

> Live in harmony with one another. Do not be haughty, but associate with the lowly. Never be conceited. Repay no one evil for evil, but give

thought to do what is honorable in the sight of all. If possible, so far as it depends on you, live peaceably with all. Beloved, never avenge yourselves, but leave it to the wrath of God, for it is written, "Vengeance is mine, I will repay, says the Lord." To the contrary, "if your enemy is hungry, feed him; if he is thirsty, give him something to drink; for by so doing you will heap burning coals on his head. Do not be overcome by evil, but overcome evil with good.

Meek leaders never get stuck in food fights with people who oppose or offend them. Instead, they are free to move their lives forward without draining their emotions, energies, and time in retaliation and retribution. Meek leaders find a blessed release when they "turn the other cheek." When they avoid the trap of getting bogged down in the relational quagmire of "an eye for an eye and a tooth for a tooth."

One of my all-time favorite passages on managing conflicts is found in Psalm 37. It reads,

> Fret not yourself because of evildoers; be not envious of wrongdoers!
> … Trust in the LORD, and do good; … Refrain from anger, and forsake
> wrath! Fret not yourself; it tends only to evil. For the evildoers shall be
> cut off, but those who wait for the LORD shall inherit the land.… the
> meek shall inherit the land and delight themselves in abundant peace
> (Ps. 37:1, 3, 8 – 9, 11).

This is not to say that meekness means that our corporate and or ministerial responsibilities are neglected. Will a leader have to release someone from their job, hold employees responsible for good work ethics and productivity, have serious and even intense talks with wayward colleagues? Of course! But the meek will do it in a way that is kind, considerate, sensitive, and just.

Will there be times when we should seek ways to reconcile with our enemies so that we can turn turmoil into peace? Of course! Seeking to reconcile would put our lives in alignment with one of the kingdom competencies that Jesus prescribed when he said, "Blessed are the peacemakers, for they shall be called sons of God" (Matt. 5:9).

When our kids were small, Martie and I were traveling to a conference to hear one of my favorite preachers. Halfway there, we were stuck in gridlock on the highway, which threatened to make us too late to attend the session that we had been looking forward to. I pulled out a map in desperation to see if we could get off the highway and find an alternate route. While my stress mounted, our son was teasing our baby daughter in the back seat; he was laughing, and she was screaming. Instinctively, I turned and hit little Joe on the forehead with the map and told him to quit making little Libby cry. Wide-eyed, he sobbingly said, "Dad, it's not be ye kind to hit people!"

We had taught him Ephesians 4:32: "Be ye kind one to another, tender hearted, forgiving one another, even as God for Christ's sake has forgiven you" (KJV). I like to think that this verse is the national anthem of the meek. Meek leaders remember that it is never "Be ye kind to hit people!" People can hit you, but you don't hit back. Rather, we trust the hitter to God, love the hitter back, and get on with the work we are called to do.

So, for all of us who have thought that meekness is weakness, it's time to think again. It seems to me that it takes a very strong leader to refuse the easy way of controlling the environment with brutish behavior. Anyone can do that. Only those who are committed to character-driven leadership will be willing to do the hard work of being the poster child in their organization for the kingdom virtue of meekness.

Kingdom leaders lead with kingdom competencies. Unlikely competencies such as being reliant, readily repentant, non-retaliatory, kind, and considerate.

But what should a leader do when she is faced with a situation in which it is to her advantage to be less than honest? When it seems convenient to sweep a wrong under the rug, when it seems more productive to look the other way when wrong is being done or when people are being maligned and abused? What does a leader do when right feels wrong and what is wrong seems like a great solution?

A PASSION FOR WHAT IS RIGHT

"Blessed are those who hunger and thirst for righteousness, for they shall be satisfied" (Matt. 5:6).

My college psychology professor would often say in his laborious Southern drawl, "Do right till the stars fall!" Maximum leaders live tethered to what is right from God's point of view … regardless. They are determined to make righteous decisions. They strive to keep right relationships with friend and foe alike, as well as to advocate for what is right for the poor and the oppressed.

It's important to note that Jesus uses words such as *hungering* and *thirsting* to describe those who live for righteousness. There is no more basic drive in a human being than the drive for food and drink. Jesus uses these images to help us understand that our desire for righteousness is an inner desire that should consume our hearts and control our heads. This is not the language of duty; it's the language of raw, primal desire. Kingdom leaders are passionate for what is right, they hunger for truth, they thirst for justice, they long for righteousness. They live to do what is right.

The Hebrew word for righteousness means "to be consistent with a true standard." A picture of this comes from Deuteronomy 25:13 – 16. The nation of Israel is reproved for using unrighteous weights in the marketplace. Imagine that you had paid for a pound of meat, but the butcher had tinkered with the weights on the scales so you only received fourteen ounces, yet paid for all sixteen. The scales were out of sync with what was right when they were intended to represent an accurate standard for measurement.

Just as the marketplace needs righteous standards for measuring meat, character-driven leaders must also have a righteous standard — an accurate basis for making judgments. The righteous standard for the character-driven leader is the Word of God, particularly as it is embodied in the life of Jesus. For every situation we face, whether in our personal life or our leadership, God's Word articulates a clear standard that must drive and define all that we are and do as leaders.

LIVING UP TO OUR POSITION IN CHRIST

Scripture teaches that we have been made righteous in the sight of God by the finished work of Christ on our behalf. That's extraordinary news! Yet, while we are righteous positionally because we are hidden in Christ, we are nevertheless called to live up to that position every day in response to God's lavish grace. Leaders who seek to lead from a platform of righteousness are living examples of what Jesus has made them to be in him. Leaders who lead unrighteously — who have their finger on the scales — betray the redemptive purpose of their Savior. They seek to gain for themselves at the expense of another, and they bring the name of Christ into disrepute.

Most leaders begin with lofty goals. Sooner or later, however, there is pressure to compromise. The seductions of recognition, applause, affirmation, wealth, and fame; the thrill of competing and conquering, of building the biggest and best empire — these temptations threaten to co-opt the way we do God's business. There is a drive to be published, to be in everyone's ear buds, to be the most-followed blogger, or to be the sweetheart of the media machine. These drives can crowd out what should be the fundamental passion of a kingdom leader: hungering and thirsting for righteousness.

As we begin to hunger for self-promoting, self-enhancing advantages, we displace the inner God-given hunger for righteousness. We feed ourselves with lesser, self-serving passions and are tempted to cheat so we can satisfy them. It's easy to compromise what is right for a quick, easy opportunity to get ahead.

Every leader faces this tension between the passionate pursuit of results and the restraints that "doing what is right" places on achieving those results. Doing the *right* thing can often slow down the process; it may even threaten to derail the outcome. So, thinking that it doesn't really make that much difference, we cheat around the edges — a little here, a little there — which soon creates a habit of compromise. And eventually, the accumulation of these habits erodes a leader's integrity.

All leaders must decide if they will be guided by righteousness or by their own self-serving desires. Choosing the latter has far-reaching ramifications. When it becomes evident to those around the leader that he is willing to cheat on what is clearly right, his moral authority is seriously compromised. A leader may be successful at getting things done, but if the process is tainted with less-than-righteous attitudes and actions, they lose the respect of those they work with, and the product is often viewed with memories of the less-than-honorable way it was achieved. Even worse, what if members of the community at large become witnesses — or more seriously, victims — of the leader's unrighteous behavior? A leader must carefully weigh the consequences of defaming the name of Christ by bad behavior in the "neighborhood" of the community at large. Which is no doubt why Paul says in his qualifications for leaders that they "must be above reproach, . . . well thought of by outsiders, so that he may not fall into disgrace, into a snare of the devil" (1 Tim. 3:2, 7).

Compromising righteousness will also have an effect on a leader's own sense of well-being. If I have chosen pragmatism over principle, then I will never be entirely confident that I am doing exactly what God wants me to do. I will have doubt if I am really working with the blessing of God or with the pragmatic process of my own manipulative strategies. I will be haunted by guilt and tangled in webs of trying to excuse myself and cover my tracks.

By contrast, acting righteously brings the reward of a clear conscience, which brings with it a great sense of security.

Jesus' call — for an all-consuming desire for righteousness — forces a leader to make a strategic, directional choice. Will I be a pragmatic, self-navigational leader, or will the right ways of the standards of God drive my personal and leadership actions and attitudes? Regardless!

On a trip out of the country, I ended up sitting next to a lawyer who, come to find out, was from the town in which I grew up, and in fact we discovered that we were in the same class in high school. During our conversation he asked, "Did you say your name was Stillwell?"

I said, "No, it's Stowell. Why do you ask?"

He said, "I have a client by the name Stillwell."

One of the leading business people in my dad's church was Art Stillwell. He ran a mega car dealership in northern New Jersey and was well known in the community. Since the lawyer and I had discovered that we had a lot in common already, I ventured to ask, "Is it Art Stillwell?" To my surprise, his answer was, "Yes!"

He then went on to say something that I will never forget. He said, "I have no other client like Art Stillwell. Most people, when they get in a bind, tell me to do whatever it takes to get them out of trouble. Art always says to me, 'Do what is right!'"

Righteous leaders reject the destructive pragmatism that elevates personal goals over godliness and hunger and thirst for righteousness as a means of accomplishing God's dreams through them.

CHAPTER 12

MERCIFUL AND PURE

Dealing with Enemies
Without and Within

It seems strange to me that Jonah would refuse to go to Nineveh (see Jonah 1:3). After all, he was God's lead prophet who had been anointed for the task of being God's spokesman. With that kind of leadership profile, I would expect Jonah to have immediately packed his bags, tucked his Torah under his arm, and taken off to do God's bidding. But that didn't happen.

It would seem logical to assume that he was afraid to go. Nineveh was the capital of the Assyrians, a people known for their unrestrained violence. He may have had visions of being treated the way they usually treated their enemies. Of being splayed alive and having his skin nailed to the city gate.

I wouldn't blame Jonah for being afraid. Personally, I'd rather be thrown overboard into a turbulent sea than have my skin peeled off. But that was not the reason he rebelled and headed off in the opposite direction.

As we now know, eventually God forced Jonah's hand and redirected him to Nineveh, where the prophet preached God's message of impending judgment. Surprisingly, Nineveh repented and begged for God's mercy. Then, shortly after his amazing success in bringing Nineveh to its knees in repentance, we find the prophet outside the city sulking over the fact that God had mercifully forgiven Nineveh's sin. In his mind, the Ninevites deserved God's judgment, and nothing short of that would do for Jonah. After all, they were Israel's chief enemy and major military threat. In a blue funk, Jonah finally comes to terms with the fact that God is not going to destroy the Ninevites, and it is at this point that Jonah admits to us why he didn't want to go to Nineveh in the first place:

> "O LORD, is not this what I said when I was yet in my country? That is why I made haste to flee to Tarshish; for I knew that you are a gracious God and merciful, slow to anger and abounding in steadfast love, and relenting from disaster" (4:2).

In other words, Jonah refused to obey God, not because he was afraid of the Assyrians, but because he had no interest in being a part of extending mercy to the wicked pagans in Nineveh. And knowing God as he did, he was afraid that that was exactly what would happen. In short, he was not willing to be a middleman in a mercy transaction between God and his enemies.

Mercy is the aspect of meekness that focuses singularly on our enemies. Leadership spawns enemies. It's an occupational hazard. So the issue is not whether you have them. The real issue is how you will deal with those who oppose or offend you. There are two options: You can leverage your power and fight back — the "eye for an eye" drill — or you can bring the ethics of the Kingdom to bear on the situation by becoming a "middleman" in a mercy transaction between God and your enemies. If you choose the Kingdom way, it will go a long way toward making you "pure in heart."

A MERCIFUL LEADER

"Blessed are the merciful, for they shall receive mercy" (Matt. 5:7).

Mercy is the grace that withholds deserved consequences. Mercy is the gift of the second chance. Mercy patiently endures and hopes for the best. Mercy forgives. Mercy refuses to retaliate. Thankfully, mercy is what God covers us with every day. As the book of Lamentations reminds us, "The steadfast love of the LORD never ceases; his mercies never come to an end; they are new every morning; great is your faithfulness" (Lam. 3:22 – 23). I hate to think of where I would be if it weren't for the "every morning mercies" of the Lord!

But extending mercy is not something we naturally do. Leaders are often jealous for their own profiles, leading by inspiring people's admiration. But enemies erode that admiration and at times threaten a leader's power base. Enemies expose a leader's faults and flaws. Enemies round up people to oppose the leader. Yet, as leaders we have the power of our position to do battle and to prevail. In fact, if our opposition is too threatening, we can:

- Preach against them. Sundays are a wonderful time to weave into our sermons the faults of those who oppose us.
- Use our "bully platform" (elder meetings, staff meetings, announcement time, and any other platform where we can address the conflict) to articulate the struggle we are having and spin the details to rally the sympathy of the others to the fact that we are being unjustly treated. If people feel sorry for us, they may turn against those who are causing the problem. It's the "martyr" routine.
- Speak freely about our opposition's shortcomings in an effort to discredit them.
- Cover our own faults by transferring the blame, and demand that our opponents seek our forgiveness for what they have done.
- Use our power advantage to exclude these enemies from the enterprise as examples of what happens to those who are "disloyal" and oppose us.

But lashing out at our critics directly or subtly finding ways to undercut them not only runs the risk of making us look small-minded and defensive, but just may also block God's work in our lives. I wonder if it ever crosses our mind that opposition may actually be God's way of catching our attention so that he can refine us through the reproof. Focusing on the offender and not pausing to hear what God is saying to us in the offense distracts us from the opportunity to discern God's hand in the situation and to cooperate with a divine purpose that in the end is for our benefit and God's glory.

I love the story in 2 Samuel 16:6 – 13. As King David rides down the road with his entourage, Shimei comes running out of the forest shouting curses at David while taking great delight in pelting the king with rocks. David's loyal follower Abishai offers to go after Shimei and cut off his head for his open acts of dishonor toward the king. Surprisingly, David responds that perhaps the Lord had brought Shimei to curse him that day, that perhaps God was trying to get his attention. There would be no beheadings for the public shaming of the king.

David sets a pattern for us. Merciful kingdom leaders withhold retaliation so that they can keep their hearts open to God's agenda in the offense.

God has a way of using deep offenses to accomplish things that could otherwise never happen. For instance, God may want to use the offense to reposition our lives for greater effectiveness. Joseph was treated brutally by his brothers. But the hidden fact in the brutality is the reality that God needed him in Egypt and that the only way this could happen was through the cruel offense of his brothers. Ascending to great power, Joseph would be used by God to rescue the Messiah seed from starvation. With that in mind, Joseph mercifully forgave his brothers and said, "You meant evil against me, but God meant it for good" (Gen. 50:20). Joseph was able to forgive his brothers because he viewed what they had done through the wider perspective of God's good purposes for his life.

Jesus is, of course, the best example of this. While dying on the cross, Jesus could have pulled all his power levers to wipe out his enemies. Instead, he prayed, "Father, forgive them, for they know not what they do!" (Luke 23:34). If Jesus had fought back, resisting the injustice of the cross, he would have negated God's plan of redemption for lost sinners. Instead, he chose to plead for mercy on behalf of his enemies, and through his death he positioned himself to play the key role in God's redemptive rescue of fallen mankind.

At the very least, kingdom leaders press the pause button and seek to see God's hand before the beheadings begin. And in fact, when we understand the full meaning of merciful leadership, revenge is never an option.

So it's no wonder that Jesus highlights the importance of mercy in his Sermon on the Mount when he says, "You have heard that it was said,

'You shall love your neighbor and hate your enemy.' But I say to you, Love your enemies and pray for those who persecute you" (Matt. 5:43 – 44). He goes on to explain why: "So that you may be sons of your Father who is in heaven. For he makes his sun to rise on the evil and the good, and sends rain on the just and the unjust" (vv. 44 – 45). If God is willing to mercifully bless his enemies, why are we ramping up for warfare?

It's clear in Scripture that mercy not only withholds retaliation, but actively forgives the offender. In Matthew 18, Peter asks Jesus, "How often will my brother sin against me, and I forgive him? As many as seven times?" (v. 21). Clearly, Peter understands that forgiveness should be his first response toward a brother who has sinned against him. But then he puts on his bean-counter visor and envisions a magnanimous offer of forgiving seven times. He hopes, I imagine, that when he reaches a number-eight opportunity for forgiveness, he can be free to beat the tar out of his enemy instead. Peter assumes that mercy has limits!

But Jesus responds by telling Peter to get a bigger abacus. He commands Peter to forgive each offense 490 times. In effect, this means that *mercy has no limits*. Forgiveness is a limitless grace that we extend no matter what. That's a tough order, unless we understand the reason we forgive others. No one *deserves* mercy, which is exactly the point! It wouldn't be mercy if our enemy *deserved* it. We are able to extend mercy to others because we ourselves have been shown mercy we did not deserve, mercy for a far greater offense than the ones committed against us. If we have been forgiven much, why would we not extend the same grace to others in order to be like our Father in heaven?

It is in this context that Jesus responds to Peter's bean-counter approach to mercy with a story that reflects Jesus' deep-seated feelings about people who refuse to be merciful when they have received great mercy (Matt. 18:23 – 32).

To make his point, he said that there was a master who had many servants who owed him money. Needling to settle up, he called in one servant who owed him ten thousand talents (which in those days was far more than Warren Buffett has in his bank account). Because the servant was unable to pay, the master told him that he was going to sell him, his wife, and children into slavery to recover his loss. The servant begged and pleaded for more time to pay, and remarkably, the master took pity on him. In fact, he forgave the servant *all* of his debt, a debt he could not have possibly repaid.

Jesus relates that, freed from his obligation to repay this enormous debt, the forgiven servant went to someone who was in debt to him. It wasn't all that much, really. Perhaps a few hundred dollars — certainly nothing compared to the millions he had been forgiven. In anger, he seized the man who owed him and choked him. His debtor pleaded for more time to pay, but the servant refused and threw him in the slammer to be tortured until he could repay the debt.

When the forgiving master heard about the behavior of the servant he had forgiven, he was furious. "You wicked servant!" he said (which is something I never want to hear my Master say to me), "I forgave you all that debt because you pleaded with me. And should you not have had mercy on your fellow servant, as I have had mercy on you?" (vv. 32 – 33).

The point is profoundly clear: God has shown us great mercy. A debt we could never have repaid has been wiped off our account. And how should we respond to this incredible act of mercy? By extending that mercy to others. Not because they deserve it, but because we have been recipients of God's abundant, *undeserved* mercy, and as such, we should be willing to do for others what God has mercifully done for us. Deep in the heart of God there is a wide streak of mercy he extends in abundant and lavish ways to all. If we are his servants, he expects us to treat people the way he has treated us, to be merciful as he is merciful.

Extending the mercy that God has extended to us makes us a "middleman" in a mercy transaction between God and unworthy sinners. And even if it does nothing to change how our enemies act, the benefits to the merciful are significant. Extending mercy frees us from the "no win" emotional entanglements of actions such as retaliation and revenge. Mercy shields us from the damaging effect of bitterness. And, mercy frees us from our preoccupation with the petty offenses that distract and preoccupy our mental energies. Best of all, our gratitude for the great mercy we have received drives us to be a living demonstration of God's great mercy that otherwise goes unexperienced in an "I don't get mad, I just get even" world.

Jesus' conclusion to the story makes for a sobering warning. "In anger his master delivered him to the jailers, until he should pay all his debt"

(v. 34). More terrifying still is Jesus' conclusion to the story: "So also my heavenly Father will do to every one of you, if you do not forgive your brother from your heart" (v. 35). Frankly, I'm not sure what that means technically in terms of what God will do if I do not show mercy, but what I do know for sure is that I never want to be on that side of the story.

I have a friend who has been struggling with a complicated situation involving massive debt. You can imagine my surprise when he forwarded me this copy of an email that he sent to everyone who owed him money. After detailing the story of the wicked servant who refused to forgive the debts of others, he wrote:[10]

> Anna and I have recently been forgiven a large debt we owed. God, over a 4-year-long process of incredible pain and huge pressure, has answered our prayers and the prayers of many, to allow us to move from what appeared to be an insurmountable debt, similar to that of the wicked servant. We have done our part and have promised before God not to allow ourselves back in any position like this again, and now see, understand and have experienced the incredible burden of living a life in debt. We have made a new promise, a covenant to God, never to be in this debt situation again.
>
> In addition we do not want to be like the servant. We are so thankful to God, mainly for the unbelievable Gift and forgiveness of our spiritual Debt through trusting our lives to Jesus, but also for the financial burden that has been lifted. We do not want to be like the wicked servant, and we firmly believe God has asked us to forgive all of the debts that anyone owes us. Thus, we are canceling all of the debts owed to us personally or through our business accounts.
>
> This is not just an earthly "Pay It Forward" deal. It is a result of the real, incredible, undeserving thankfulness to God providing salvation through trusting our hearts to Jesus Christ by his sacrifice and canceling our debt of sin. It is also the result of His answer to years of prayer for providing a way out of our financial burden from which we have been rescued. We pray that through this experience and story you will also take a much deeper look at what God's total and complete forgiveness looks like!
>
> May God bless you all greatly in 2013!

---

10. Email quoted by permission of the sender.

The thing that I love about my friend's extension of mercy to others is that it provided him with a great opportunity to highlight the richness of God's mercy. Acts of mercy provide windows for others not only to see our mercy, but to see beyond to the mercy of God.

At this point it would be easy to object, "But they haven't sought my forgiveness. I'll extend mercy when they ask for it." The truth is that Jesus finished the work of forgiveness on the cross long before we even knew we needed it, let alone asked for it. We forgive *because* we are forgiven, not because someone has asked us to. And if we have already forgiven others in our hearts, we will be ready and prepared when and if they do ask for it.

But can you ever forget? If that seems impossible to you, you are right. It is impossible to forgive and *forget* an offense simply by an act of the will. What we can do, however, is learn to attach new meanings to our memories. Joseph did not forget that his brothers had wronged him. Instead, he attached a whole new meaning to their actions. When he thought about their brutal betrayal, he marked that thought with the insight that God had intended it for good.

Memories can haunt us or help us. Over time, they can help us if we can learn to attach to the memory the truth that God will use it to build our character (James 1), to bring about that which is good (Romans 8:28), or for any other agenda that he knew could only happen through an offensive scenario. These kinds of mental Post-It notes attached to our memories make our memories meaningful.

Is there a time when those who offend and oppose you need to be dealt with by the proper authorities? Certainly. When laws are broken and crimes are committed, that should be reported. Elders and board members should protect and defend leaders against their enemies. But at the end of the day, our mercy needs to be present as an incarnation of the mercy of God, even when earthly justice must still be served.

My favorite ride at the county fair was always "Dodge 'Em!"—more commonly known as bumper cars. You paid your quarter and climbed aboard a little buggy poised to be driven in an arena overcrowded with other drivers in their own little buggies. You knew you were going to get bumped — you just didn't know when or how hard. When someone bumped you, you'd hit the accelerator and chase them down to smack them in return. Which means, of course, that he then took aim to do the same to you. That may be a great strategy for bumper cars, but it's a terrible strategy for leadership or for life — especially if you are trying to pursue a leadership style that reflects kingdom values.

Jesus offers a better option: Be merciful! Mercy means that forgiveness trumps revenge. It believes that an unfailing trust in God to deal with my enemies trumps the downward dynamics of protecting myself by giving people what I think they deserve.

If the character-driven leader is committed to "how" she leads — humbly reliant, readily repentant, consistently meek, passionately righteous, and unwaveringly merciful — then the next profile of maximum leadership will mark the kingdom way of why she leads.

PURE IN HEART

"Blessed are the pure in heart, for they shall see God" (Matt. 5:8).

Our "heart," according to the Bible, is the operational center of who we are and what we do. It's like the motherboard of life. It's where we dream, desire, deliberate, and decide. It's where motives reside that determine direction and define decisions. And because we all have a heart, the question is, What kind of a heart does a character-driven leader need to have? In Jesus' terms, a leader needs to lead from a "pure heart" if he or she is to reflect the priority competencies of the kingdom. So what does that look like?

To be pure, our hearts need to be free of the debris that clutters and contaminates much of our leadership instincts. Pure hearts don't lead for personal gain, fame, wealth, applause, or the thrill of goals and dreams accomplished. Pure-hearted leaders keep a vigilant eye on unrighteous thoughts, attitudes, and actions that pollute them at the core. They know that keeping the pollutants out means that they need to be proactive in filling their hearts with all that is pure and right so that there is no room left for the toxic presence of the impulses and instincts of Satan's kingdom.

I am struck by the way Jesus reproves the leaders of the churches in Ephesus and Laodicea in the book of Revelation. Leadership patterns in both churches were less than pure, and in both cases the problem had to do with their rejection of the role Jesus played in their leadership. Jesus' words to them indicate that purity begins with *who* we permit to be the driving force in our hearts.

As we have seen, in his letter to the elders of the church in Ephesus, Jesus notes that he has something against them. Why? Because they have "abandoned the love [they] had at first" (2:4). By "first," Jesus does not mean first in time, but rather the kind of love they had as their first priority. To put it another way, they no longer were "doing church" out of a love for Jesus as their primary motivation. Interestingly, this was what many would think was a successful church. Jesus notes that they had worked hard and patiently endured suffering in a hostile cultural environment. They were intolerant of evil and diligent in testing teachers for sound doctrine. If you didn't know better, you might even nominate them for the Church of the Year award!

Yet Jesus commands them to "Repent, and do the things you did at first" (v. 5). If they do not repent, Jesus warns that he "will come … and remove your lampstand from its place" (v. 5). Although they outwardly appeared to be successful, the lack of doing ministry with the right motives, from a pure heart, put the church at odds with Jesus. That's a sobering thought.

While purity of the heart has many dynamics, it does force us to come to grips with the purity of our motives. It forces us to think about *why* we do what we do. Many motives drive a leader's life. But Jesus wants our primary motive for doing all we do to be out of our love for him. All that we do should first be an act of love and worship. Why do we preach? Why do we plan, set goals, and cast vision? Why do we get up every morning and go to our post to carry out our duties? Why do we dream about bigger and better success? Why are we willing to be reliant, repentant, meek, righteous, and meaningful? If the answer is anything other than wanting to serve to express our love to Jesus, then we are opening the doors of our hearts to toxic contaminates.

When we lead as an act of love to Jesus, leadership becomes an act of worship. We lead because Jesus is worthy of the expenditure of our gifts and talents, and we happily elevate him as Lord over the domain we manage. When we lead as an act of worship, we lead to honor him and not ourselves. We lead to advance his cause and his dreams and not our own. Leadership as an act of loving worship means our will is surrendered to his will, our ways to his ways, and our thoughts to his perfect wisdom.

Our work is no longer about us, but always about him. Seeing leadership as an act of love and worship annihilates the threat of pride, greed, and self-promotion.

When I lead for Jesus' sake, it empowers me to work above the irritations of annoying people. My leadership is not for them; it is for Christ, who never annoys me! It guards me from the temptation to lead in unrighteous ways, because I would never do wrong as an act of love to Jesus. It forces me to give him the glory for all of my accomplishments, because I have done it all for him!

Leading from the "heart motivation" of love and worship to our worthy Shepherd and Servant-King is a purifying influence in a leader's heart.

But there is another aspect of pure-hearted leadership that is reflected in Jesus' words to the church at Laodicea. That city sat at the intersection of major trade routes, so it became an affluent center of world trade. The Laodiceans were known for their gold, their medicinal eye salve, and their rich, woolen garments. These products made Laodicea a wealthy place to live, which cultivated a self-sufficient spirit among its citizens. In their affluence they needed nothing and needed no one's help. So much so that after a major earthquake devastated their city in the first century, they refused financial aid from Rome. "We don't need your help," they said. "We can rebuild with our own resources."

The Laodiceans were competent, successful, affluent, and prone to say, "I need nothing" (3:17), which meant, of course, that the Christians there who were caught up in this self-sufficient cultural attitude thought they didn't even need Jesus. In fact, that is exactly what concerned Jesus. When he wrote to them concerning how offensive their attitude was toward him, he said that the reason was, "For you say, I am rich, I have prospered, and I need nothing…" (Rev. 3:17).

This left Jesus standing outside the door of their hearts (v. 20), excluded from center stage in their lives. Jesus said that their self-sufficient attitude made him sick and that from his point of view, they were not " … in need of nothing," but without him at the center, they were actually "wretched, pitiable, poor, blind, and naked" (v. 17).

As we have already seen, leaders who lead from a sense of self-sufficiency suffer from a deception that pollutes their hearts. They lead believing that their successes are a direct result of their prowess as leaders.

Self-consumed, self-sufficient leaders stand at the center of their universe, leaving Jesus standing outside.

Biblical sanity reminds us that any success we achieve is not really our success, but is a gift of God's favor. We do not deserve the applause; he does. We do not deserve material rewards; he is the reward that outshines any material outcome. We should be surprised that he grants us the privilege of being successful for him in the first place; not proud and self-sufficient.

Jesus wants us to serve from the motivation of how desperately we need him. And so, as he did with the Ephesian and Laodicean leaders, he calls us to repent. And he reminds us as well that he stands at the door of our hearts and desires to come in to fellowship with us and to cleanse our hearts from the motives that dishonor him and discount our leadership.

I wonder, amid the busyness and self-centered focus of our leadership, if we can hear him knocking.

Pure-hearted leaders hear his knock and welcome Jesus into the inner sanctum of their hearts. The highest good and joy of our lives as character-driven leaders is to serve him as an act of love and worship and to reliantly fellowship with him as we watch with great delight all he is willing to do through the gifts and opportunities with which he has lavishly blessed us.

Think of the power of a leader whose life and leading is marked by reliance on God, repentance, meekness, righteousness, mercy, and purity of heart. This kind of leadership will not only advance the kingdom, but also bless the leader with the advantage of a moral authority that guarantees the fulfillment of God's vision through the leader's life.

Of all the habits of a character-driven leader's life —

- Prioritizing character as the primary goal of a leader's life,
- Embracing the transformational identity of a follower of Jesus,
- Seeking to lead from the platform of moral authority,
- Leading as a shepherd,
- Leading as a servant,
- Leading from a pure heart that is God-reliant, repentant, meek, and righteous

— there is no habit more encompassing for kingdom success than the habit of living and leading to magnify Christ!

A REDEFINED EXPECTATION

What Do You Expect?

I recall asking a counselor what the recurring core issues were that tended to unravel life and bring people to his couch. Because I'm in the people business, I thought it might be helpful to know. He surprised me when he said the list of root issues was quite short, but that near the top of that list was *broken expectations*. He noted that he consistently found that his clients would engage life with high expectations as they entered into marriages, careers, and friendships — only to have the high expectations dashed and their dreams destroyed. And when that happened, a whole host of destructive dynamics would dismantle their sense of stability and well-being. These clients, he said, commonly struggled with anger, bitterness, hatred, disillusionment, despair — even suicidal thoughts.

Leaders, especially aspiring leaders, enter the field of their calling with high expectations. On the list of usual expectations is that, given their giftedness, they will eventually end up in a good place. And given how charming they are, that the people they serve will like, love, affirm, and reward them. But after a period of time, they find they are stuck in a challenging place with some really difficult people. After years of faithful service they are still leading in a small church where the only speaking invitation they get is for devotions at the monthly seniors group in their own church. Unheralded, unrecognized, and unaffirmed, it's easy for these leaders to languish when they feel they are stuck in a place of limited ministry and influence. Particularly if they are stuck with people who are less than encouraging and at worst oppositional.

When his or her expectations are dashed, what does a character-driven leader do?

I find it interesting that Paul himself was stuck in a really bad place, surrounded by some less-than-wonderful people. Given his circumstances, you would think that his spirit would be in the dumps and that feelings of disappointment and despair would have him grumbling about how he got stuck in that place with people like that. But surprisingly, he was in good spirits — in fact, elated — in spite of his place and the people he had to deal with.

The place is house arrest in Rome, and the people are believers in Rome who flat out don't like Paul. They are being spiteful in carrying out their work, hoping to add to his affliction.

Paul shares his testimony with the Philippians and gives us a clue as to why he can be where he'd rather not be but still be positive and why he can be with people like the Roman believers but still rejoice. He writes to them,

> I want you to know, brothers, that what has happened to me has really served to advance the gospel, so that it has become known throughout the whole imperial guard and to all the rest that my imprisonment is for Christ. And most of the brothers, having become confident in the Lord by my imprisonment, are much more bold to speak the word without fear....
>
> In every way, ... Christ is proclaimed, and in that I rejoice.... For to me to live is Christ, and to die is gain (Phil. 1:12–14, 18, 21).

You can't beat the optimistic tone! What's the secret?

Being the global leader of the church, personally appointed by Christ himself, Paul now finds his ministry restricted in the confines of house arrest. He tells the Philippians, however, that this is all turning out for good, because the whole imperial guard knows he is there for the sake of the gospel. When I tie that in with his concluding remarks in Philippians 4:22, where he says, "All the saints greet you, especially those of Caesar's household," it seems as if something amazing is going on.

I find myself wondering, *Could it be that one of the guards assigned to him asked what a nice guy like him was doing in a place like that?* And instead of griping about it, which may have been our response, he told the guard that he was there for preaching the resurrection of Christ in the synagogues … which is exactly why he was in prison. No doubt, the guard would have connected the dots with what he had heard about that amazing event when some of his colleagues were guarding Jesus' tomb. As Paul unfolds the whole story and the meaning behind it, the guard bows his knee to Christ. Having accepted Jesus, the guard goes on break and tells his buddies that he has just heard the whole story about this Jesus of Nazareth. He encourages them to take his shift so they can hear it firsthand as well. Soon there are "saints" in Caesar's household!

Paul may be stuck in a bad place with a seemingly restricted ministry, but in that place God has given him an unusual mission field and influence in a sphere he would never have dreamed of.

So, I wonder, for those of us who find ourselves stuck in a bad place, if it has ever crossed our minds that God has put us where we are on purpose, *for* a purpose? And that as we faithfully pursue our leadership as a follower of Jesus, he will prosper our work in his way and in his time for unusual and unexpected outcomes? It might be well to remember the story of Pastor White, who led my dad to the Lord. Seemingly stuck in a small and unheralded ministry, he faithfully labored for outcomes that were far-reaching long after he had gone on to heaven. My mother-in-law sent me a birthday card when I was in my thirties (now ancient history). On the inside it said, "Bloom where you are planted!" Great leadership advice.

Well, if the place doesn't get you, there is a good chance that your expectation about people will. Being stuck with less-than-encouraging people is an ongoing challenge for every leader. I would have expected that, given Paul's position in the church and all that he had done to advance the gospel, the believers in Rome would have rallied around his imprisonment and done all they could to support him. All-night prayer meetings, notes, hot dinners … the love should have been flowing in lots of special ways. But, as he says,

> Some indeed preach Christ from envy and rivalry, but others from good
> will. The latter do it out of love, knowing that I am put here for the
> defense of the gospel. The former proclaim Christ out of selfish ambi-
> tion, not sincerely but thinking to afflict me in my imprisonment (Phil.
> 1:15 – 17).

Thankfully, some of the believers were on his team! There will
always be a few on your team: children in the church, your spouse, and
your golden retriever! But then there will always be those who seem set to
oppose leaders regardless. Why the brothers in Rome were out on Paul is
hard to know. Maybe they were tired of him getting all the headlines, of
telling them how to do church. Maybe some of them had written letters
that never got read in church. It's hard to figure, but nevertheless, they so
disliked him that they were hoping through their success in preaching the
gospel that they would add to his affliction. One thing is clear, they were
now doing ministry out of a spirit of rivalry and selfish ambition.

Paul has lots of options to vent his broken expectation: use his pen
to rebuke them, talk to others about them, call the elders who supported
him together to chart out the discipline process. Unexpectedly, however,
Paul writes, "What then? Only that in every way, whether in pretense or in
truth, Christ is proclaimed, and in that I rejoice" (Phil. 1:18). Where does
a response like that come from?

We are all well aware that this competitive spirit in ministry did not
die in the first century. Whether it is someone in the church competing for
the limelight or other churches or organizations trying to outdo everyone
else, the demons of doing Christ's work out of *envy and rivalry* remain
alive and well. Interestingly, Paul refuses to get into the mud pit with them
and finds his joy in the fact that the gospel is advancing.

I recall hearing Andy Stanley tell a story at a Moody Founder's Week
Conference that, quite frankly, sounds like fiction. To accommodate
their growing ministry, his church moved out to the edge of Atlanta and
acquired a large tract of land. His only misgiving was that down the street
there was a small Vineyard church. But because there were no other location options, they proceeded, and before long, there were Sunday morning
traffic jams in the neighborhood, and the church had overcrowded parking lots.

Soon after their arrival, Andy got a message that the pastor of the Vineyard church had called. Fearing that he would get an earful, he nonetheless returned the call. The Vineyard pastor said, "Pastor Stanley, welcome to the neighborhood. We have been praying for years that God would reach this part of Atlanta with the gospel, and *you are the answer to our prayers!* In fact, I noticed that your parking lots are overflowing. We have plenty of room in ours. Feel free to have your people park here if it's helpful." It is clear that in Atlanta there is at least one character-driven leader who knows that we weren't called to kingdom work to compete against each other but to go arm in arm against the forces of hell, whose gates will not prevail against us!

So here Paul is, stuck in a less than wonderful place with some very annoying people. And his spirits are high and encouraged. What is his secret? If he can give us a clue, we will be well on our way to handling our own broken expectations, victoriously.

Paul shares his secret when he writes,

> Yes, and I will rejoice, for I know that through your prayers and the help of the Spirit of Jesus Christ this will turn out for my deliverance, as it is my eager expectation and hope that I will not be at all ashamed, but that with full courage now as always Christ will be honored in my body, whether by life or by death. For to me to live is Christ, and to die is gain (Phil. 1:18 – 21).

He has one *eager expectation*: that Christ will be honored in his body whether by life or death. He hasn't brought to his leadership the expectation of being in a great place or being well liked or, for that matter, any other expectations, except that (as some Bible versions put it), Jesus will be "magnified" through him — wherever he is or whoever he is with. He knows he can magnify Jesus in house arrest and in his interactions with oppositional people. So when he gets opportunities to do that, he is elated! Expectation fulfilled.

Honoring Jesus regardless is one expectation that is manageable. We are normally victims of broken expectations; it's what others do to us. This is an expectation we can manage to ultimate success. Seeking to honor Jesus through our lives wherever we are and whoever we are with is always possible.

With this as his only and eager expectation, it's no wonder Paul writes, "For me to live is Christ ... !" (Phil. 1:21).

Magnifying Jesus means that we make him large, visible, and present in every event and encounter. It's demonstrating his love, mercy, grace, patience, justice, and any other relevant expression of Jesus. So in a bad place with less-than-encouraging people, Paul eagerly expects to make Jesus large.

This is an important word for us. We have a tendency of getting in the way of Jesus. Of revealing more of "me" than of him. Of seeking to magnify myself, my dreams, and my aspirations. Of expecting others to magnify me as well.

Many of us have been to sporting events where people in front of us keep standing up, blocking our view. Eventually someone yells, "Will you please sit down? I can't see the game!" I wonder if people we serve and lead ever want to say to us, "Please sit down. I can't see Jesus!"

Several years ago, I was scheduled to fly to Grand Rapids to speak at a conference later that day, only to discover upon reaching the county airport that the plane scheduled to take me there couldn't land at the airport due to weather conditions. That meant there was no way I was going to get to the speaking engagement that day. Sadly, my response in that little airport was less than admirable as I complained with great intensity to the gate agent (who was also the baggage person and air traffic controller) that he should have found a way to get the plane down as I commiserated about the dilemma this had put me in ... as though he could do anything about it.

To my embarrassment, he said, "You're a minister, aren't you?" to which I sheepishly said yes.

"Then God will take care of you!" was his painful reply!

I picked up my bag and started to walk out of the airport when I remembered that one of my church members had just said to me a couple of weeks earlier that if I ever wanted to go somewhere, he would be glad to fly me there. I picked up the phone and called him. He happily said that the weather was not a problem for taking off and that he would meet me at hangar #9 in twenty minutes. I hung up the phone and caught the ticket-taker-baggage-air-traffic-controller out of the corner of my eye and felt so ashamed.

How different it would have been if I had awakened that morning with one eager expectation: to magnify Christ! Had I done that, I might have said to the traffic controller as he unsuccessfully tried to get the plane to land, "I really need to get to Grand Rapids, but I've been a follower of Jesus for years and my life is in his hands. He will make a way if it is in his will, but if he doesn't, I am happy to rest in his plans for my day." If I had said something like that, I could have gone back to the counter with the rest of the story ... to the glory of God. Instead, I had woken up that morning with one eager expectation: to get to Grand Rapids.

How different it would be for all of us if we got "me" out of the way and lived with one eager expectation: That wherever we are or whomever we are with, Christ will be magnified through us!

Making Jesus large is the ultimate outcome of character-driven leadership — the ultimate outcome for leaders who say, "For me, to lead is Christ!"

ZONDERVAN®